IT Service Management with FitSM Version 3

Other publications by Van Haren Publishing

Van Haren Publishing (VHP) specializes in titles on Best Practices, methods and standards within four domains:

- IT and IT Management
- Architecture (Enterprise and IT)
- Business Management and
- Project Management

Van Haren Publishing is also publishing on behalf of leading organizations and companies: BRMI, CA, Centre Henri Tudor, CATS CM, Gaming Works, IACCM, IAOP, IFDC, Innovation Value Institute, IPMA-NL, ITSqc, NAF, KNVI, PMI-NL, PON, The Open Group, The SOX Institute.

Topics are (per domain):

IT and IT Management
ABC of ICT
ASL®
CMMI®
COBIT®
e-CF
FitSM
ISM
ISO/IEC 20000
ISO/IEC 27001/27002
ISPL
IT4IT®
IT-CMF™
IT Service CMM
ITIL®
MOF
MSF
NIS2
SABSA
SAF
SIAM™
TRIM
VeriSM™
XLA®

Enterprise Architecture
ArchiMate®
GEA®
Novius Architectuur Methode
TOGAF®

Project Management
A4-Projectmanagement
DSDM/Atern
ICB / NCB
ISO 21500
MINCE®
M_o_R®
MSP®
P3O®
PMBOK® Guide
Praxis®
PRINCE2®

Business Management
BABOK® Guide
BIAN®
BiSL® and BiSL® Next
BRMBOK™
BTF
CATS CM®
DID®
EFQM
eSCM
IACCM
ISA-95
ISO 9000/9001
OPBOK
SixSigma
SOX
SqEME®

For the latest information on VHP publications, visit our website: www.vanharen.net.

IT Service Management with FitSM Version 3

A practical and lightweight framework for IT

Van Haren
PUBLISHING

Colophon

Title:	IT Service Management with FitSM Version 3
Subtitle:	A practical and lightweight framework for IT
Authors:	Anselm Rohrer, Dierk Soellner
Reviewers:	Dr. Michael Brenner and Dr. Thomas Schaaf (for the original German version)
Publisher:	Van Haren Publishing, 's-Hertogenbosch-NL www.vanharen.net
DTP and cover design:	Coco Bookmedia, Amersfoort-NL
ISBN Hard copy:	978 94 018 1252 8
ISBN eBook (pdf):	978 94 018 1253 5
ISBN ePub:	978 94 018 1254 2
Edition:	First edition, first impression, February 2025
Copyright:	Van Haren Publishing, 2025

Trademarks

COBIT® is a trademark of ISACA.
FitSM® is a trademark of ITEMO e.V.
ITIL® is a trademark of Axelos Limited.

Foreword

I have watched for 40 years as organizations struggle to gain the hoped-for value from an investment in ITSM best practices, such as ITIL. Organizations make the same mistakes again and again with each adoption of the latest shiny new best practice framework. Often it is unclear why they are being adopted; there is a poor understanding of where to start; they are not applied in an end-to-end approach; employees are not engaged in designing the working practices; the adoptions are often oversized for what is needed; smaller organizations struggle with the size and complexity of the frameworks and, all importantly in my mind, adoptions are mostly not embedded in a culture of continual improvement. There is an expression "Cannot see the wood for the trees", meaning that people focus too much on the details of something and so they do not notice what is important about the thing as a whole, which is a common characteristic for the failures mentioned above.

Is FitSM the next Shiny New thing and will we make the same mistakes again?

In this book, and the subsequent practical follow up book, Anselm Rohrer and Dierk Soellner draw upon their extensive experiences in small and medium sized organizations to provide a 'practical and application-oriented path' to address the challenges mentioned above. The approach is based upon 82 concise requirements and draws upon ISO/IEC 20000, COBIT and ITIL for content. These requirements help organizations see through the details into what is important. The author's motto, drawn from FitSM, seems to be "keep it simple", describing 'what' needs to be done, and focusing on 14 core processes – reducing the size and complexity of an ITSM adoption. As the authors stress, those requiring more can look to ITIL, COBIT or other extensive frameworks.

For the authors the strength of the FitSM approach lies in the focus on the 'requirements' to be met for a functioning IT service management system, supported by the 'maturity assessment' that provides a reference point for continual improvement. Continual improvement in my mind, and endorsed by the authors, needs to be a core capability. Yet according to my global survey, 76% score this as a 'Weak' to 'Poor' capability. Based upon findings from the assessment, the authors then recommend improving maturity

"In small steps with small changes", with an emphasis on addressing the all-important 'People' factor, which I believe is the number one success or fail factor for adopting best practices. These small improvements are enabled by an easy-to-implement, simply structured approach, backed up by a role model, templates and implementation guides. The implementation guidance will appear in the follow up book to this publication.

Another strength lies in presenting the processes in a value-stream oriented way which fits in with a growing market shift towards value stream thinking and more agile ways of working. FitSM scopes the following value streams: Offer and Agree, Plan and Ensure, Monitor and Roll out, Eliminate and Prevent, Report and Improve, Protect and Secure and maps the 14 core processes across these value streams.

With recent shifts towards agile and DevOps ways of working, more organizations are adopting 'principles' to drive the all-important behaviors underpinning these new ways of working. I identified three core common principles shared by agile, DevOps, Lean and ITIL4 – these being 'Focus on value', 'Collaboration and flow' and 'Continual learning and improving'. FitSM aligns powerfully with these, the authors placing an emphasis on what they label as systematic IT service management, focusing on 'Service and customer orientation', 'Process orientation', and 'Continual improvement' – once again, an example of focusing on what is important. This systematic approach is supported by the basic FitSM principles of the FitSM approach: Practical, Consistent, Sufficient and Expandable.

I am also delighted to see that the authors stress the importance of Governance, Customer Relationship Management and Service Portfolio Management. In my global surveys a massive 80% scored these as 'Weak' to 'Poor' capabilities, underpinning our long-standing poor alignment to business needs and priorities. This lack of alignment to business priorities has been the top scoring 'Attitude, Behavior and Culture (ABC)' worst practice chosen in global workshops for 15 years in a row!

Finally, the success of FitSM, as with any approach, stands or falls on the 'people' factor. Translating FitSM into sustainable, repeatable, desirable behaviors, underpinned by an organization-wide culture of continual improvement is the basic prerequisite for sustainable success. The authors have clearly stressed the importance of engaging people in an approach of continual improvement.

Embracing the philosophy of continual improvement, what I would like to see added to the next iteration of FitSM, is to extend the training and certification from the theoretical foundation and advanced courses, to more practice- and evidence-based certifications, adding as a requirement the adoption of an approach such as the 8-Field model to ensure that training outcomes are scoped up-front and are measured afterwards, to demonstrate the value from a training investment. Our global survey figures match findings from a Harvard study revealing that only 12% apply new skills learned in

Learning & Development programs to their jobs, and only 25% believe that training measurably improved performance. Combining a training approach like this, with the practical guidance from the authors, would be a recipe for continued success.

Paul Wilkinson

Foreword of the authors

More than ever, the support of business processes by IT systems and applications is characterized by a high degree of penetration and dependency of operational processes. The use of IT ensures efficient work, increases productivity and often makes new business models possible in the first place. Large organizations and professional IT service providers have been focusing for years on establishing IT service management (for clarification of terms, see Section 2.1 IT service management). Defining processes based on best practice approaches makes it possible to provide IT services professionally.

When applying IT service management frameworks such as ITIL, small and medium-sized IT organizations in business and public administration face the challenge of distilling out the relevant parts for their own organization and transferring them into practical use with little effort. Often, those responsible have neither the financial resources nor the time to successfully complete this task. Thus, it's often the case that oversized process models are applied, complicated processes are implemented, unsuitable specifications are made, or examples and templates are used 'blindly' without the necessary adaptation. This problem has intensified with ITIL Version 4.

FitSM emerged from an EU-funded project, which was launched in part to help small and medium-sized businesses adopt best practices by right-sizing them for their organization using a continual improvement methodology. References to a "lean, lightweight approach" are more effective than a focus on organizational size as they are useful to everyone. EU funding ensures free availability after the end of the project, as the results must be made available to the general public free of charge. The history of the project is described in Section 1.1 History of FitSM.

Target audience

This book is aimed at the following audiences:

- IT managers who want to establish high-quality, but at the same time lean and efficient IT processes.
- IT managers who want to evaluate the quality of their IT department according to objective criteria.

- IT employees who take on, or are expected to take on, organizational tasks in the future.
- IT staff, who are expected to place their own activities in the overall context in order to optimize them towards the organizational goal.
- Leaders of IT service companies who want to provide customer-optimized IT services and, if necessary, are looking for a way to have this certified.
- People who want to prepare for one of the FitSM certification exams, especially the Foundation and Advanced exams.

Motivation for the book

FitSM has been a standard for IT service management for small and medium-sized enterprises since 2014. With this book, we have created a complete work from the various parts so that the target audience has a consistent entry point. In this way, we would intend to address the need for a complete work on simple IT service management and make the manual compilation of information from various PDF documents superfluous. Anyone interested in FitSM will now find further practical tips and, of course, all relevant information on FitSM sensibly compiled.

Objective

This book bundles the individual components of the FitSM family into a cohesive body of work. This turns a collection of important official sub-documents into a coherent presentation of a lightweight approach to IT service management that:

- Is based on important terms (FitSM-0);
- Includes the goals and activities of the proposed processes (FitSM-2);
- Provides a generic role model (FitSM-3);
- Incorporates the requirements for IT service management (FitSM-1) and the characteristics in terms of a maturity model (FitSM-6).

A framework is described that shows small and medium-sized IT organizations in clear and practicable ways how to meet their current challenges. In doing so, we have linked the requirements from FitSM-1 as the central basis of FitSM in the chapters with the associated capability levels from FitSM-6. The practical example, which runs like a thread through the individual chapters, was important to us. This makes the suggestions and contents of FitSM more tangible for use in the operational world. This practical example also integrates elements from FitSM-4 (providing templates and examples) and FitSM-5 (providing selected implementation guides). These two areas are not part of the core of FitSM, but are very helpful for its practical application.

Perhaps you are among the people who believe that another framework for IT service management is not necessary and that simply omitting individual elements would not make such a framework any easier or more useful to use. However, the experience of the two authors from training and consulting mandates shows that many managers and employees in small and medium-sized IT departments lack a truly usable and practice-oriented approach. Even in larger organizations, FitSM can now be used to make IT service management more understandable and assist in its implementation. Furthermore, in times when DevOps is increasingly finding its way into companies, FitSM can be a great help in practically implementing IT service management within agile teams. FitSM provides a practical path for IT service management, especially in these smaller IT organizations. Instead of extensive process descriptions and further detailed proposals, it shows the IT manager what needs to be achieved on the basis of transparent requirements. These requirements are based on the ITSM standard ISO 20000 and specify the goal, which can then be addressed by the IT department. Instead of working through many pages of best practice, we show the most important elements and enable the reader to develop himself and his area of responsibility step-by-step.

How to work with this book

This book explains the basics of FitSM. Among other things, it brings together the aspects of the various original documents thematically in a simple, consistent and readable form. The second book *FitSM – A practical implementation guide* contains practical examples and tips for its implementation in IT organizations. This first book provides an understanding of the FitSM framework. It helps the individual reader to build up knowledge about FitSM. In the second book, questions about the introduction of FitSM are clarified, i.e. FitSM is presented in the context of organization-wide use.

If you want to strengthen your knowledge right away, you can read both books simultaneously. First the theoretical basics in this book and immediately afterwards the corresponding chapter for the practical implementation. Of course, it is also possible to read this book completely first and the book *FitSM – A practical implementation guide* afterwards. For those who simply want to pass the exam, the contents of this book are enough.

Structure

First, we provide an introduction to FitSM as well as basic concepts and terms in this book. This is followed by a description of the general requirements with which FitSM identifies overarching aspects of successful IT service management. This is followed by a roughly structured description of FitSM's 14 processes, each of which is combined with the associated roles and the requirements.

The description of the processes always follows the same structure. At the beginning, the goal or the main task of the process is presented in a few sentences. This is followed by the process description and an explanation of the most important process-specific roles from FitSM-3. The requirements for the process from FitSM-1 are then listed. The terms and phrases used within these requirements are already explained in the process description. For each of the requirements, the capability levels are considered. This illustrates what is important for an effective and efficient implementation of the process.

Practical implementation (second book)
The second book offers a practical guide to FitSM implementation with invaluable insights for organizations looking to adopt this IT service management framework efficiently. The book provides a wealth of actionable tips and best practices, distilled from real-world experiences, to help readers navigate the complexities of FitSM adoption. Through detailed case studies of two distinct organizations, it illustrates the versatility and adaptability of FitSM across different business contexts, offering readers a blueprint for using the framework to meet their specific needs. By combining practical advice with concrete examples, this book serves as an indispensable resource for IT professionals and managers, enabling them to swiftly and effectively implement FitSM within their own organizations.

Acknowledgements
Even though both authors have many years of experience in the field of IT service management, such a work cannot be done without broad professional support. With the objective of putting our experience and the resulting knowledge together with the FitSM standard in such a way that it offers real value for the readers from the perspective of small and medium-sized IT organizations, we have deliberately set the bar high.

We would therefore like to take this opportunity to thank those people who have made significant contributions to this book: Dr. Michael Brenner and Dr. Thomas Schaaf assisted in the technical editing for the German edition in 2016 and provided valuable comments as well as contributing the chapters on the history of FitSM and the description of the federation-based approach. It was important to both authors that this support provided an official acknowledgement from the FitSM project and the active working group. Finally, due to the generous permission of the association ITEMO e.V. as the rights holder of FitSM to use the logo and the word mark, we believe our book will be seen and used as the standard work on FitSM.

Both authors would like to take this opportunity to thank their wives and daughters for their moral support. Both families have always struck a healthy balance for us. On one hand, they gave (and still give) us space and time for our passion in IT service management and "going the extra mile", whilst on the other hand, they permanently provide distance to it. They help us to clear our heads, gain distance and enjoy life.

For better readability, a more masculine spelling ("process manager") is used in this book. We have tried to use gender-neutral terms in places where reading comfort is not affected.

Contact

The world of IT service management is still in motion. Both authors have permanent contacts in practice, which open up new questions and other perspectives. With this exchange, which is supported by publications, projects and lectures, a lightweight approach can be continually developed. The website *fitsm.online* offers further information and current references. Contributions are regularly published on topics that cannot find space in a reference book of this kind.

With this book, we would like to open up another source of contact. We would be happy to hear your opinion about FitSM and this book, or about practical IT service management in general. Take the opportunity to tell us your questions and challenges, to discuss them together and to work out solutions. You can reach us in different ways:

email	Anselm.Rohrer@rohrer.info	Dierk.Soellner@dierksoellner.de
LinkedIn	linkedin.com/in/anselm-rohrer/	linkedin.com/in/dierksoellner/

Contents

1 Introduction

Business processes in companies are increasingly dependent on working information technology. The IT departments of large companies have long since recognized this fact and are endeavoring to align their operations with proven processes and organize themselves within the framework of IT service management. The need to reduce downtime, plan and implement changes or integrate external service providers in a targeted manner is growing. This affects IT departments in small and medium-sized companies as well as in public administration. The same applies to IT service providers who offer and bill companies for their services. Their customers are also demanding more reliable services and, increasingly, the provision of agreed services instead of project work on a 'time and materials' basis.

All of the organizations mentioned – just like the IT within large organizations – are faced with the growing challenge of organizing IT more in line with customer requirements and building up a reliable organization and a changed quality awareness in addition to enhancing the technical expertise of their own staff. However, they are often faced with the problem that the frameworks developed for larger organizations, such as ITIL and ISO/IEC 20000, are too powerful and complex for their needs or make excessive demands. IT managers of many mid-sized companies consider the established ITIL framework to be too complex, or even completely deny its suitability for mid-sized companies.[1,2] This is where FitSM comes in. The most important components of established frameworks were worked out and consolidated under the principle "Keep it simple" to the most necessary. FitSM aims to improve things in the right places. In contrast to classical approaches, FitSM focuses on describing 'what' needs to be done. The 'how' is left to practical implementation and can thus be adapted to individual conditions.

1 Study by *msg* services ag with participation of nearly 300 companies.

2 Note by the authors: Statements about other frameworks in IT service management are to be seen in the respective context and are not meant to be generally judgmental. All established frameworks, especially ITIL and ISO/IEC 20000, have their advantages and have earned their current status. Knowledge of these frameworks is also useful for an approach according to FitSM. Therefore, they have been integrated into this book in many places, especially in Section 1.4 Related standards and frameworks.

FitSM refers to a framework for practical IT service management (ITSM) that is licensed under the Creative Commons License (CC License) and is therefore free and open for use. This chapter first describes the development of FitSM. This is followed by an overview of the components of FitSM, before content-related benefits are discussed.

1.1 HISTORY OF FitSM

The first version of FitSM was developed between 2012 and 2015 as part of a project from the European Commission's Seventh Framework Program (FP7). The primary goal of this project, entitled "Service Management in Federated e-Infrastructures" (in short: FedSM[3]), was initially to support three European providers of IT services in the field of research in improving their IT service management. Most research institutions operate their own data centers, but very few have sufficient capacity to provide their users with the amount of resources needed for specific experiments or calculations. Over time, therefore, closely networked federations have emerged, often hidden behind buzzwords such as 'grid computing', 'e-infrastructure' or 'eScience'. During the work in the 'FedSM' project, the formative idea of a federative approach emerged. Therefore, the working group decided to call the framework they developed 'FitSM'. The 'F' stands for federative, so that 'FitSM' can be described as an approach for federative IT service management.

While in the past technical development progressed relatively quickly through networking and the coupling of systems and resources via special software, the need for (process) organizational development was underestimated in many places.

Example: When several smaller IT service providers join forces with their respective data centers to collaboratively provide IT services for their customers and users, the management of disruptions (incidents) must also be coordinated. Who should users contact in the event of an incident? What are the information flows and escalations between the players involved? And how quickly do incidents have to be resolved? What level of availability and reliability is required?

The FedSM project was not a classic research project, but a so-called "Coordination & Support Action". The main challenges that had to be overcome can be summarized as follows:

- The use of decentralized data centers and infrastructures as the basis for highly networked and federated services.
- The lack of awareness of the need for IT service management processes in many places.
- A strong focus on technology with low organizational maturity.

---

3 Further information on the FedSM project is provided by CORDIS, the European Community Research and Development Information Service: https://cordis.europa.eu/project/rcn/104760/de.

The following prerequisites were identified as key success factors for the successful introduction of IT service management:

- Lean, lightweight approach based on the simplest possible process model and clear requirements as targets.
- Practical implementation with the help of easy-to-use descriptions of activities and roles as well as easily adaptable documentation templates.
- Consideration of situations where service delivery occurs as part of a federation, i.e., an association of multiple providers.

These factors remain the essential features of FitSM to this day. Ultimately, FitSM was a consolidated result of the implementation of IT service management by the organizations involved in the aforementioned project. Experienced practitioners, managers and scientists from many different European countries were involved in the creation of FitSM.

During the project, it became apparent that the resulting model was also of interest to other organizations where the desire for simple procedures without excessive administrative effort was prevalent. The standard was published under the name FitSM and the rights were transferred to the ITEMO e.V. (IT Education Management Organization) association at the end of the project.

Today, FitSM is maintained and developed by this non-profit association. Topics such as the further development of the standard, translations, maintenance of the website, development of the community, and training and certification are dealt with in various working groups. These working groups consist of the participants in the FedSM project and other experts from the ITSM community. All of the work is being done with the understanding that FitSM will remain freely available to everyone in the future. This includes all components of the standard as well as the training material provided.

1.2 THE STRUCTURE OF FitSM

FitSM as a framework is composed of individual standards. In essence, there are four documents. They are supplemented by application aids.[4]

FitSM standard/core (FitSM-0 to 3)
FitSM-0 provides a brief overview of the overall FitSM construct. It defines all technical terms used in FitSM in a simple way. This creates a uniform understanding of the terms used. The practical use of this document as a glossary has proven successful.

4 The individual standards can be downloaded from the official FitSM website: https://fitsm.itemo.org

The definitions from the existing ITIL and ISO/IEC 20000 frameworks were largely considered in the descriptions of the terms in order to avoid any contradictions.

FitSM-1 contains requirements for a functioning IT service management system. The document is divided into a part with general requirements and a part with process-specific requirements.

FitSM-2 recommends various principles and activities that help to implement the requirements of FitSM-1. These are not mandatory requirements, but rather recommendations for action that facilitate compliance with the requirements. To simplify the assignment of recommended actions to requirements, FitSM-2 contains the same structure as FitSM-1.

FitSM-3 describes a role model that builds on the requirements of FitSM-1. Responsibilities and tasks of individual roles are defined, and recommendations are made for the possible assignments of roles to persons.

Implementation aids (FitSM-4 to 6)
The core of FitSM with the content specifications and descriptions is completed by practice-oriented supplements:

FitSM-4 provides templates and examples for various documents so that they do not have to be developed from scratch in every organization. For example, templates for process definition or a service level agreement can be found here. These documents are explained in detail in the second book on the practical implementation of FitSM.

FitSM-5 contains guides to support the implementation of IT service management and some processes. These documents are also explained in detail in the second book on the practical implementation of FitSM.

FitSM-6 provides an assessment tool for evaluating the IT service management maturity level of an organization. It helps to determine in which areas the set goals have been achieved and where further expansion of the organization's own capabilities would be useful.

While FitSM-0 and 1 show what is needed to achieve goals and continual improvement, FitSM-2 and 3 help to organize and realize this. FitSM-4 and 5 bring examples and instructions, i.e. support the implementation, and FitSM-6 shows the current degree of implementation. The actual core is represented by FitSM-0 to 3, while FitSM-4 to 6 support the implementation.

To be considered FitSM-compliant, organizations must only meet the requirements in FitSM-1. These are normative, i.e. mandatory, requirements. All others are of an

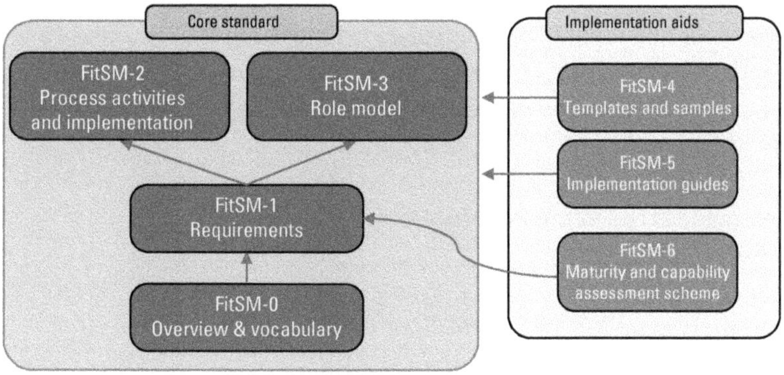

Figure 1: FitSM – Structure and components

informative nature only. The introduction of processes or roles in accordance with FitSM is not mandatory if the requirements of FitSM-1 can also be achieved in another way.

1.3 FitSM AS A LIGHTWEIGHT APPROACH

FitSM contains components from ITIL, ISO/IEC 20000 and COBIT. These were reduced and merged. However, the advantages of FitSM do not lie solely in the reduction of processes or roles. Therefore, some useful differences to existing frameworks will be discussed at this point.

Service management system
FitSM formulates its own quality management system on the basis of ISO 20000, including a commitment and responsibility for management and the regulation of document control. This facilitates its adaptation in smaller companies, particularly because of the systematic and structured view.

Practicable determination of the actual state
The requirements from FitSM-1, in conjunction with the assessment tool (FitSM-6) for maturity assessment, provide a practicable determination of the actual state as a basis for implementation and orientation in ITSM. A step-by-step and clear view is promoted and a manageable starting point for continual improvement is established.

Simple structure of FitSM
The most relevant difference between existing frameworks and FitSM lies in the underlying approach. While the ITSM standards developed over the years provide a whole series of best practices that have been increasingly expanded, refined and formulated over time, FitSM is very simply structured and can be quickly understood and grasped. It deliberately does not claim to be best practice, since the focus is on describing the requirements to be achieved.

FitSM represents an easy-to-implement, free basic solution for getting started with ITSM, especially for small and medium-sized IT organizations. For many IT organizations, achieving a high level of maturity for the defined requirements is already a meaningful but nonetheless costly project task.

FitSM's process model includes the following processes:

- Service Portfolio Management (SPM);
- Service Level Management (SLM);
- Service Reporting Management (SRM);
- Service Availability & Continuity Management (SACM);
- Capacity Management (CAPM);
- Information Security Management (ISM);
- Customer Relationship Management (CRM);
- Supplier Relationship Management (SUPPM);
- Incident & Service Request Management (ISRM);
- Problem Management (PM);
- Configuration Management (CONFM);
- Change Management (CHM);
- Release & Deployment Management (RDM);
- Continual Service Improvement Management (CSI).

Unlike other frameworks for IT service management, FitSM does not graphically represent these processes in any structure with sequences, dependencies or a lifecycle in the original documents. From a content perspective, however, the processes can be represented as follows. This seems to be more understandable and comprehensible.

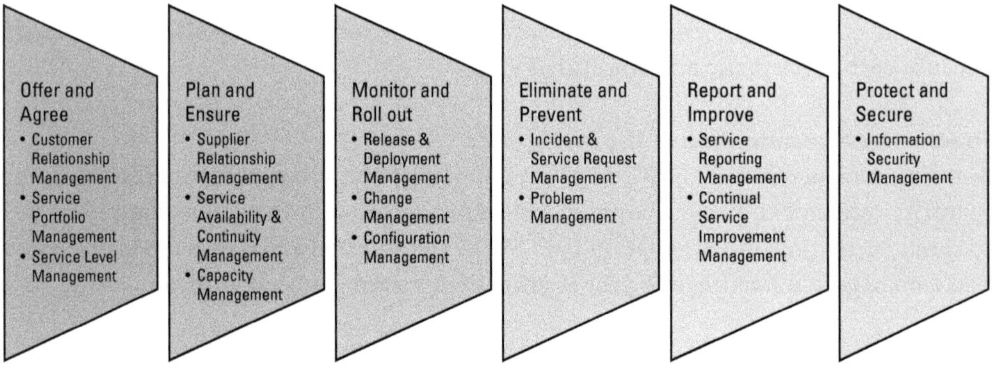

Figure 2: FitSM processes at a glance

Scope

With FitSM, small and medium-sized IT organizations can ensure a concrete review and measurability of the maturity level through the integrated requirements. With FitSM, IT managers are provided with a clear list of requirements and can use the easily understood descriptions to determine the maturity levels themselves. Furthermore, the requirements for activities to achieve the next maturity level can be derived.

Company organization and size
Smaller and medium-sized IT departments do not need many of the contents and processes of the existing frameworks, or do not need them to the same extent. For example, too much formalization often does not fit in with the culture of a small, well-established team, and the number of employees means that too many roles do not make sense.

A look at the IT service management processes introduced in practice shows that it is precisely the processes described in FitSM that were mentioned most frequently, whilst aspects such as strategic planning and detailed financial considerations of IT are rarely implemented across the board. One reason for this is certainly that smaller and medium-sized IT organizations cover these tasks by integrating them into the processes within the company.

The small number of ITSM elements (processes, roles, documents, etc.) in FitSM is also useful for small and medium-sized IT organizations. The federation approach is interesting for all organizations in which IT services are achieved through collaboration between different individual organizations.

Applicability
IT organizations can start with FitSM and take advantage of the benefits and offerings of the more comprehensive IT service management frameworks as needed. If, for example, the training content of FitSM is not sufficient, the more advanced training courses of other approaches can provide more detailed information. If an IT organization needs further examples and suggestions on the content of processes for specific processes, then the respective methods can be used as a supplement.

Central requirements
FitSM offers direct support for the adaptation of ITSM. Clear and unambiguous descriptions of the requirements to be achieved help to promote self-motivation and the goal of self-improvement. In this respect, the assessment tool included in FitSM-6 offers a very usable support for an organization's own assessment. With FitSM, the current maturity level of the service provider can be determined individually. The implementation is supported by the definition of sub-goals/steps.

In contrast to CMMI as a recognized and comprehensive maturity model, FitSM gets by with three maturity levels[5]. Achieving the highest maturity level in a process is rather simple compared to other maturity models, but sufficient for small and

5 We do not include level 0 (Non-existent) because there is no awareness of the task or the required outcome, i.e. it is practically non-existent. The assessment tool for FitSM-6 includes the ability levels 1-3.

medium-sized IT organizations. At this point, we distinguish between the capability levels of the individual requirements, analogous to FitSM, which then converge to form a corresponding maturity level for the process (see also the terms in the Glossary).

The following detailed descriptions can be seen for the respective stages:

Level 0: Non-existent
The process is not needed. The task that is to be completed by the process does not exist.

Level 1: Ad-hoc/Initial
One is aware of the task, but it is not controlled or there are some relevant results in which, however, core elements are missing. The essential tasks are performed in an uncoordinated manner.

Level 2: Repeatable/Partial
Tasks are repeatable but not formally defined, results are only partially complete.

Level 3: Defined/Complete
Tasks are well-defined and deliverables are complete; responsibilities for both are defined and documented.

The higher the capability level, the more coordinated the processes. The proportion of improvisation and 'reaction' decreases. However, as the level of capability increases, so does the level of management and documentation.

1.4 PRINCIPLES OF THE FitSM APPROACH

FitSM is guided by four key principles in the management of IT services and three key principles for systematic IT service management.

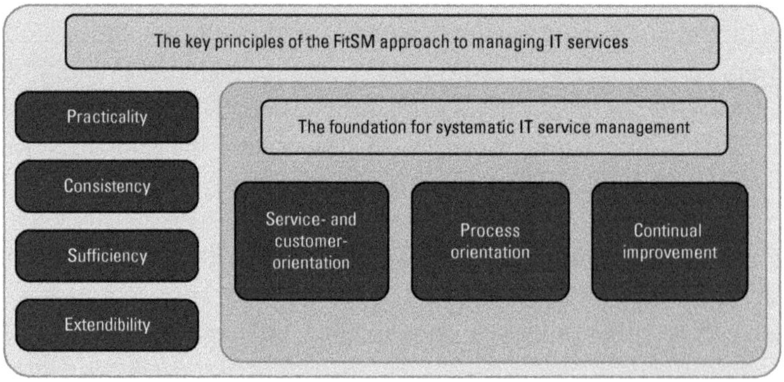

Figure 3: Key principles for IT service management and FitSM

Practical IT service management
In IT service management, practical means that it is better for a system to be 'good' as well as working than it is for it to be 'perfect' and continually in the planning stage. This refers to an approach to ITSM that aims to reduce the complexity and cost of ITSM implementations by tailoring them to an organization's needs and reducing them to the essentials.

Unlike comprehensive ITSM implementations that may include all aspects of ITIL, COBIT, or other frameworks, practical ITSM focuses on implementing the key processes (driven by requirements in FitSM) and best practices that matter to an organization.

A practical ITSM implementation also considers the size and complexity of an organization as well as its resources and requirements. Such an implementation can achieve the benefits of ITSM, such as improved service quality, higher customer satisfaction and greater efficiency and effectiveness, without investing too much time and resources in the use of frameworks. In other words: FitSM focuses on sufficient implementation of ITSM practices.

It is important to note, however, that from FitSM's perspective, a practical ITSM implementation need not be less robust or comprehensive than an all-inclusive implementation of other frameworks. Instead, FitSM focuses on the implementation of requirements and their maturity levels to ensure that the organization can reap the benefits of ITSM without getting bogged down in details or incurring unnecessary costs.

Consistent IT service management
'Consistent' in IT service management means assigning roles and ensuring that tasks are performed in a steady manner. Optimization and detailed documentation can follow. This refers to the application and execution of ITSM practices and processes in an organization through a systematic and consistent manner. It is important that ITSM is applied consistently across an organization to ensure that IT services are delivered in a reliable and high-quality manner.

Consistent ITSM implementation includes, among other things, standardizing the processes for delivering IT services so that they are clear and understandable to all stakeholders. This is often achieved through consistent policies and procedures for practices and processes to ensure that the entire organization works in the same way. Communication and collaboration are also important in this context. Clear and open communication between all stakeholders (service providers and customers) is important to ensure that everyone has the same understanding and that IT services are delivered consistently.

Consistent ITSM helps an organization manage its IT services more effectively and improve customer satisfaction by ensuring stable, reliable, and high-quality service delivery.

Sufficient IT service management

In IT service management, 'sufficient' means the description and application of the components of a service management system in line with requirements. Not all processes, documentation and other elements need to be in place at the outset. The implementation of ITSM practices and processes should be appropriately tailored to the needs of an organization. A sufficient ITSM implementation does not have to be complete or comprehensive, but it should meet the needs of the organization and ensure that IT services can be managed and delivered appropriately.

Sufficient ITSM includes, among other things, defining ITSM objectives aimed at improving the effectiveness and efficiency of IT services, and increasing customer satisfaction. To do this, it is helpful to identify the key processes needed to effectively manage and deliver IT services and ensure that these processes are adequately implemented. Further, a sufficient ITSM implementation should be tailored to the size of the organization and ensure that ITSM practices and processes can scale appropriately. The most important aspect of this is the establishment of continual improvement to ensure that IT services are continuously improved and optimized. This can be aptly summarized as "More important than the processes themselves is the process to improve the processes!".

Extendible IT service management

In IT service management, 'extendible' means that a start on a manageable scale helps to build capabilities and add other helpful sources of knowledge as needed. The goal is to implement ITSM practices and processes that are flexible, scalable and can adapt to an organization's changing needs. An extendible ITSM implementation must be able to keep pace with the speed of business and technology evolution in order to ensure that the organization's IT services are managed effectively and efficiently.

Extendible ITSM includes the ability to scale so that it can adapt to the size and complexity of the organization. This includes the ability to scale ITSM practices and processes to a larger or smaller number of users, services or sites. Meaningful automation is also important. An extendible ITSM implementation should be able to automate ITSM tasks and processes to improve efficiency and scalability.

Extendible ITSM is important to ensure that an organization can effectively manage and deliver its IT services while adapting to changing business and technology conditions. By implementing extendible ITSM, an organization can deliver its IT services more effectively and efficiently while improving customer satisfaction and reducing overall costs.

The foundations for systematic IT service management are:

Service and customer-orientation

IT support for customers and users is based on services with agreed service levels. These services describe the customer's expectations on the one hand and the IT service provider's offering on the other. The basis for cooperation is laid out via the joint agreement of services between the customer (as the recipient of the delivery of value) and the IT service provider (as the supplier of the value).

Process-orientation

The activities required for planning, providing, operating and controlling services are carried out within the framework of sensibly implemented processes. These processes help the IT service provider to align its work with the services, i.e. with customer expectations. They give structure to service delivery in the IT organization.

Continual improvement

The entire service management system follows the Deming approach to quality management: Plan-Do-Check-Act. This approach can be found in many IT frameworks (even in agile approaches) and again provides a structure for continual improvement. It helps to systematically identify improvement opportunities and translate this into improvement measures.

1.5 RELATED STANDARDS AND FRAMEWORKS

FitSM is based on a number of IT service management frameworks. It was derived from these under the premise of creating a simple, understandable framework that can be used practically. Knowledge of these frameworks from IT service management, as well as adjacent areas, provides the opportunity to obtain further information in a targeted manner in individual cases.

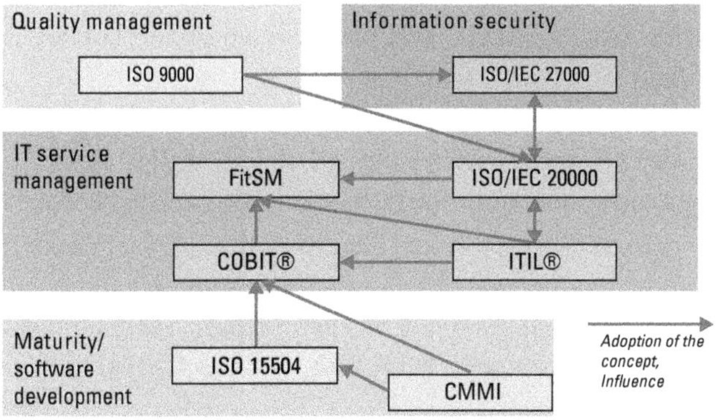

Figure 4: Related standards and frameworks in IT service management

Overview of selected standards and frameworks

In terms of content, FitSM has made use of three frameworks. The basic orientation and structure as well as the management system are based on ISO/IEC 20000. COBIT brings an intensive focus on the customer's business strategy with its emphasis on IT governance, whilst many technical contents were added from ITIL.

In quality management, ISO 9000 has become established, and its continual improvement process has found its way into ITIL, ISO/IEC 20000, and above that into FitSM.

The FitSM Information Security Management process is based on the process of the same name in ISO/IEC 20000. For the implementation of the Information Security Management process, the latter refers to ISO/IEC 27000, which describes the requirements for a functioning, holistic management system for information security.

For every process to be implemented, the question arises as to what level of maturity it should reach. If you compare this goal with the current maturity level, you can see where there is still a need for optimization. CMMI is probably the best-known maturity model. In ISO 15504, this maturity model is applied to the area of IT service management, among other things. CMMI and ISO 15504 have influenced COBIT, which in turn forms the basis for FitSM-6[6]. There, a simple procedure for assessing the maturity of the FitSM management system and processes is described.

In addition to the frameworks directly or indirectly related to FitSM, there is also EN ISO 19011 and EN ISO/IEC 17021, which define criteria for auditing a management system.

FitSM thus provides a simple and comprehensive basis for implementing an IT service management system. If a higher degree of organization is required during implementation, it may be worthwhile to look at the corresponding process in ISO/IEC 20000 or ITIL.

FitSM, requires physical, technical and organizational measures in the Information Security Management process. Annex A of ISO/IEC 27001 provides a high level of detail on the measures that may be involved.

Many organizations operate a quality management system, modeled on ISO 9001, in which case some FitSM requirements can be met quite easily by using existing procedures and systems.

If you want to know more about a maturity assessment or even have to withstand an internal audit, you can go beyond FitSM-6 and use COBIT, ISO 15504 or CMMI.

---

6 Note from the authors: ISO 15504 is no longer the appropriate reference – ISO/IEC 33xxx is a family of International Standards developed by ISO that revises the ISO/IEC 15504 series of International Standards and provides a framework for the assessment of process quality characteristics (e.g. process capability) and organizational maturity. The framework for assessment covers processes employed in the development, maintenance, and use of systems across the information technology domain and those employed in the design, transition, delivery and improvement of services. Results of assessment can be applied for improving process performance, benchmarking, or for identifying risks associated with application of the processes. (taken from the ISO website).

1.6 PRACTICAL IMPLEMENTATION

This book explains what FitSM is and how it works. In parallel, there is the book *FitSM – A practical implementation guide*, which shows examples of how FitSM can be implemented in companies and public authorities. Using two companies as examples, the FitSM processes are established step-by-step using simple tools, mechanisms and strategies. It is important to establish the necessary degree of management and control without over-managing the organization.

As a reader, you have various options for familiarizing yourself with FitSM using these books.

Are you interested in the theoretical basics of FitSM and perhaps want to take a FitSM exam? Then this book is sufficient.

Are you interested in the practical implementation and would perhaps like to introduce FitSM in your company? Then the book *FitSM – A practical implementation guide* can support you. You can read this book first and then the practical implementation guide or you can read both books in parallel: first the theoretical part of a process and then the examples of practical implementation. This allows you to deepen your understanding of the respective process. To simplify parallel reading, we have harmonized the chapter structure. For example, if you have read Section 4.1 Customer Relationship Management in this book, you will find the corresponding practical implementation in the book *FitSM – A practical implementation guide* in the same Section 4.1 Customer Relationship Management. This allows you to switch between the two books without much effort.

Enjoy reading.

2 Basic concepts and important terms

Before this book goes into more concrete detail about the contents of FitSM, important concepts and terms need to be explained. These relate to the subject area in which FitSM operates, namely services, service providers and IT service management in general.

FitSM provides a definition of all important terms via the document FitSM-0. These are listed and explained at the relevant points in this book. Initially, in a book about IT service management, this term itself must be clarified. Then we will go into essential elements of IT service management. The service management system is just as important as a formative framework as the service management plan is as the basis for implementation. The terms 'IT service' and 'service level' as well as 'IT service provider' are used to describe the basis for a fundamental understanding.

2.1 IT SERVICE MANAGEMENT

IT service management aims to develop IT organizations into customer- and service-oriented IT service providers[7]. The focus is on the IT organization's customers and their requirements. These IT organizations are referred to as IT service providers and ideally cover the requirements of the customers with the services they offer. To ensure the quality of the services, the IT service provider must organize itself accordingly. This means, the IT service provider must ensure appropriate tasks are completed consistently by using defined processes or a reference organization according to roles and the tasks they perform. These coordinate the work of all those involved with the aim of delivering services effectively and efficiently. This delivery of services should be oriented towards value for the customer, i.e., providing the customer with value in relation to undertaking their work.

FitSM defines IT service management as follows: "Entirety of activities performed by an IT service provider to plan, deliver, operate and control IT services offered to customers".

7 The terms 'IT service' and 'service' are used synonymously in the context of this book, analogously to the FitSM standard. The same applies to the terms 'IT service provider' and 'service provider'.

IT service management is therefore the management of all specialist capabilities of the IT organization to provide value for the customer in the form of services. In addition to processes, these capabilities consist of functions to plan, design, organize, monitor, and improve service delivery throughout the complete lifecycle.

An IT service provider can be an external service provider or an internal IT department of a company. The customer is usually the entire company, which uses IT services to carry out business services or processes. The operational implementation and utilization of IT service management is carried out by an IT service provider. They use the content of ITSM to operate and organize their business.

There are several frameworks and standards that support an IT service provider in introducing IT service management. Among the best known are ITIL, COBIT and ISO/IEC 20000. These three frameworks have been briefly explained in Section 1.5 Related standards and frameworks. FitSM has been developed based on these frameworks and places great emphasis on systematic IT service management (as described in Section 1.4 Principles of the FitSM approach).

2.2 SERVICE MANAGEMENT SYSTEM (SMS)

The entire management system that controls and supports service delivery is called a service management system (SMS). It describes the goals to be achieved, the processes and procedures required to achieve them, defines roles and plans resources. It also includes policies, agreements, and plans. It includes everything that the service provider needs in order to deliver services to the customer at the agreed level of quality. This means that the whole system or, in other words, the daily use of IT service management within the user organization is what matters. Whereas guidelines, for example, tend to be formulated in abstract terms and have a more general focus, procedures are drawn up for specific cases in the operational work.

In concrete terms, the SMS regulates the alignment and further development of the entire service management. It determines the customer's objectives in order to derive the service provider's objectives, align all processes with them and ensure that they are implemented in tools. It determines a person responsible for the entire SMS and assigns a process owner to each of the individual processes. It defines minimum standards for documentation and, ideally, provides document templates.

The requirements for an SMS are considered in more detail in Chapter 3 General requirements.

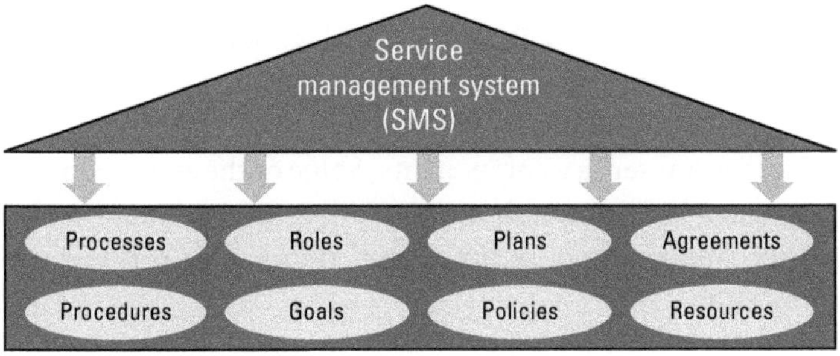

Figure 5: Contents of a service management system

2.3 SERVICE MANAGEMENT PLAN

The procedure for introducing an SMS together with realistic sub-goals are defined in the overarching service management plan. As this plan also regulates the continuous optimization of the SMS during operation, it continues to play an important role even after the introduction. Such a plan and its anchoring in the management system is an essential basis for the sustainable establishment and further development of the processes in the FitSM framework and in the IT organization.

At the beginning of the introduction of an SMS, the service management plan should be more long-term and comprehensive. It should contain a basic vision, give direction and run roughly over one to two years. The activities for an initial phase of up to three to six months should be specified in more detail. As soon as the execution of the plan has started, the service management plan can then be changed to a more agile approach. This means that the planning horizon is then shortened and operational implementation is reduced to four weeks. The service management plan then draws its content from the work of continual improvement (mostly done by the Continual Service Improvement process).

2.4 IT SERVICE, SERVICE PROVIDER AND SERVICE LEVEL

Companies, public authorities and organizations of all kinds each pursue a primary goal. While companies focus on business success, public authorities are usually concerned with sovereign tasks. Business processes are defined to achieve these goals. Parts of these business processes are supported with the help of IT services, be it through e-mail communication, accounting software, web applications or CRM systems. An IT service is a way of categorizing or framing what IT service providers offer to their customers. As a result, customers receive value, which is usually reflected in more effective and/ or more efficient means of undertaking their business processes. Furthermore, an IT service should add value to all participants in the service relationship, not only for the customer. It can incentivize process owners and managers to do it well and improve upon it. The requirements for IT services derive from the business requirements of the customer, as well as the service goals, the service description and so on.

An IT service usually consists of several service components. Some of these components enable the service, while others extend or support the service. An extension would be, for example, additional storage space, faster response times or cryptographic components for encrypted e-mail communication.

The IT service provider is responsible for providing an IT service. The IT service provider coordinates and combines the service components in such a way that the IT service delivers the expected or agreed value for the customer. The IT service provider can be an external service provider. In many cases, however, the primary target audience of FitSM is an internal IT department that may integrate individual services (services or service components) from external providers.

A disruption to a service often results in the impairment of customers' business process. Disruptions cannot be avoided completely, but they can be managed and reduced to an acceptable level. The quality objective for a service is thus derived from the quality objective of the supported business process.

The benefit of a service is determined by the value generated for a customer and the associated users. This value is composed of value from the customer's perspective (utility) and the fulfillment of a given performance promise (warranty). FitSM describes value like this: "Value should be considered as a composition of the function (fitness for purpose) and quality (fitness for use, covering sufficient availability/continuity, capacity/performance and information security) connected to a service."

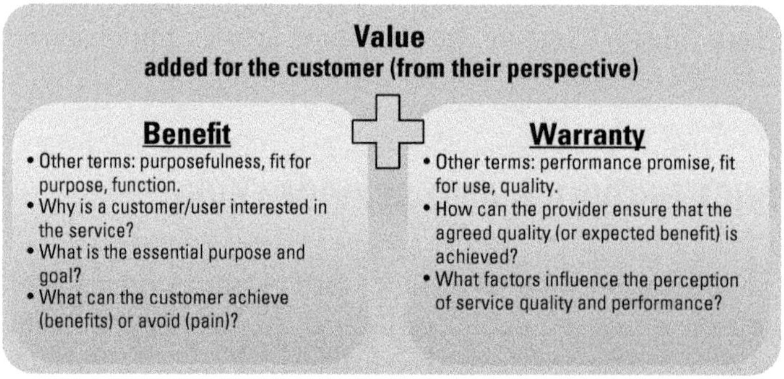

Figure 6: Value of a service

The usefulness is typically represented by the actual functionality (functional properties, what is provided in terms of performance). For example, a human resource management system should be able to manage employees, run payroll, schedule absences, or manage leave accounts.

By fulfilling a given performance promise, the agreed functionality is delivered at an agreed quality level. These are non-functional characteristics that describe quality and quantity. Typical characteristics for this are:

- Availability: What is the maximum frequency and length of time that the functionality may be unavailable or restricted?
- Capacity: How fast does the functionality need to be performed? How much storage space is required?
- Information security: Does the functionality process information that requires special protection? Does access to this information need to be specially secured?
- Continuity: Does the functionality have to be available again as quickly as possible in the event of a disaster, or can it be temporarily dispensed with in such an exceptional situation?

In addition, there are other properties, such as ergonomics, usability, accessibility, task appropriateness, expectation conformance, self-descriptiveness, controllability, fault tolerance, customizability, learning facilitation, and many more.

An IT service provider agrees with customers on a service to meet certain expansion stages, a so-called service level. The service level is defined by the goals it is to achieve. The expansion levels can be titled 'Gold', 'Silver', and 'Bronze', for example. 'Gold' is the highest level and includes a resolution time for incidents of eight hours or service availability of 99.5%. For the graduated 'Silver' service level, a resolution time of 24 hours or an availability of 98% applies. The simplest level, 'Bronze', then stipulates a resolution time of 60 hours or service availability of 95%.

Service levels are fixed in a contract known as a service level agreement (SLA) with customers in order to achieve a binding agreement on the provision and use of certain services between provider and customer. This contract can also be structured as an agreement if the customer and IT service provider are in the same organization. It is important for both sides to recognize the binding nature of the contract or agreement.

3 General requirements

FitSM-1 is a collection of all the requirements that make up a FitSM-compliant SMS. The implementation of all requirements serves as proof of the effectiveness of an SMS. These requirements are clearly formulated. However, in practice there is always room for interpretation and specific individual circumstances. For this reason, FitSM-6 formulates different levels of implementation and assigns corresponding capability levels to the requirements.

FitSM lists a total of 82 requirements that should be implemented by an organization that provides IT services to customers. These requirements are divided into two parts. The first part contains 17 general requirements (General Requirements GR) with relevance for the entire SMS. The second part is process-specific and contains the requirements for the respective processes (Process Requirements PR)[8]. The general requirements are divided into different areas and listed in the following table. The official abbreviations of the areas are given in brackets.

Area	Quantity
GR 1: Top Management Commitment & Accountability (MCA)	3
GR 2: Documentation (DOC)	4
GR 3: Scope & Stakeholders of IT Service Management (SCS)	2
GR 4: Planning IT Service Management (PLAN)	2
GR 5: Implementing IT Service Management (DO)	2
GR 6: Monitoring & Reviewing IT Service Management (CHECK)	2
GR 7: Continually Improving Service Management (ACT)	2

8 FitSM has numbered all requirements. This numbering initially consists of the abbreviation GR or the process abbreviation. This is followed by the numbering of the general requirements or the numbering of the processes. This is, in turn, followed by numbering within the general requirement or process. All 82 requirements are listed in Appendix D, sorted by page number.

The 65 process-specific requirements are distributed among the 14 processes as follows.

Process	Quantity
SPM: Service Portfolio Management (PR1)	4
SLM: Service Level Management (PR2)	5
SRM: Service Reporting Management (PR3)	3
SACM: Service Availability & Continuity Management (PR4)	4
CAPM: Capacity Management (PR5)	4
ISM: Information Security Management (PR6)	5
CRM: Customer Relationship Management (PR7)	6
SUPPM: Supplier Relationship Management (PR8)	4
ISRM: Incident & Service Request Management (PR9)	6
PM: Problem Management (PR10)	4
CONFM: Configuration Management (PR11)	5
CHM: Change Management (PR12)	6
RDM: Release and Deployment Management (PR13)	6
CSI: Continual Service Improvement Management (PR14)	3

An effective service management system in accordance with FitSM encompasses all 82 requirements, as it is not sufficient to consider only the IT-related requirements from the processes. The general requirements are covered in this chapter and the process-specific requirements in the subsequent chapters.

3.1 COMMITMENT AND RESPONSIBILITY OF TOP MANAGEMENT

When designing the service management system, ensuring governance is an important goal. Various definitions exist for the term 'governance', which can be summarized for the SMS as follows: The service provider is responsible for consistently delivering services that meet the needs of their customers at the promised level of quality. Thus, governance compliance is a top management responsibility and is codified in the first three general requirements at FitSM:

- GR 1.1: Top management takes responsibility;
- GR 1.2: Specify service management policy;
- GR 1.3: Conduct management reviews.

3.1.1 Top management takes resonsibility

FitSM demands a fundamental commitment from top management to a quality management process. This is specifically stated in the following requirement for a service management system:

The service provider's top management must clearly demonstrate that it wants to implement a service management system. This means planning, implementing, operating, monitoring, reviewing and improving the SMS. To do this, a top management person must take responsibility for the entire SMS. They can delegate tasks, including competencies and sufficient resources. However, the responsibility remains with them. If the implementation is only decided by a management team consisting of several people, there is a risk that no one really feels accountable.

Capability level	Description
1	Top management primarily deals reactively with service management issues. Within top management, there is no clear allocation of responsibilities in relation to the SMS.
2	Top management actively tries to control the SMS and its outcomes. The duties of the SMS owner usually fall to a specific member of top management, but there is no clear formal definition or assignment of the role of the SMS owner.
3	Top management actively controls the SMS. The role of the SMS owner, together with its competencies and tasks, is defined and clearly assigned to a member of top management.

3.1.2 Specify service management policy

The service management policy is a key element in FitSM and must include at least the following:

- An obligation to meet the service requirements of the customer.
- The commitment to a service-oriented approach to service management.
- A commitment to process-oriented implementation in service management.
- A commitment to continual improvement.
- Definition of, and commitment to, overarching goals for service management.

The introduction of an SMS entails some consequences. Responsibilities and competencies may shift, and the tasks and working methods of the people involved will change in some cases. This naturally leads to uncertainty and resistance among many of those affected. Therefore, it is necessary for top management to set the goals, which in this way determine the direction and the focus. The person responsible for SMS from top management must actively support the change and can turn those affected into participants to strengthen acceptance.

Capability level	Description
1	A general service management policy has been documented, at least informally. However, it lacks clear goals for service management and/or a clear commitment to all core principles of service management.
2	A general service management policy has been formally documented. It covers service management goals and a commitment to key service management principles at least in a general manner.
3	A general service management policy has been documented. It covers all the necessary elements, including clear and verifiable service management objectives, a commitment to continual improvement and a commitment to a service and process-oriented approach. The service management policy is approved by the owner of the SMS and communicated to all relevant parties.

3.1.3 Conduct management reviews

The appropriateness, maturity and efficiency of the SMS are examined as part of regular management reviews. These reviews must be conducted to verify if the guidelines and processes are target-oriented, if they are adhered to, and if they produce the desired results in terms of practical implementation. On this basis, potential for improvement can be identified and follow-up measures defined. The review is carried out by the SMS manager. Since this person is a member of top management, in practice the preparation of the management review, including decision templates, is often carried out by an employee who is more intensively involved in the daily application of the SMS.

Capability level	Description
1	The SMS owner conducts management reviews at irregular intervals. There may be long periods without a management review.
2	The intervals of the management reviews are not planned, but they reliably take place at reasonably regular intervals.
3	The owner of the SMS conducts management reviews at planned intervals. The frequency and general content of the reviews are planned. The results are documented.

3.2 TYPE AND SCOPE OF DOCUMENTATION

The foundation necessary for establishing effective service management is documentation that is comprehensible to those using it. How detailed this is in individual cases ultimately depends on how it is implemented within the company. A high level of documentation leads to clear framework conditions, but also increases the effort required to create, comply with and review these. A low level of documentation offers flexibility and reduces the effort required, but also offers greater scope for interpretation. This has a negative effect on activities that should always be carried out in the same way and makes it more difficult to measure the achievement of objectives. In principle, FitSM attaches importance to documenting not only the service management system and processes, but also the results. Four requirements are formulated in concrete terms:

- GR 2.1: Document service management system;
- GR 2.2: Create process descriptions;
- GR 2.3: Document process results;
- GR 2.4: Control documents.

3.2.1 Document service management system

To support effective planning, the basic components of the SMS must be documented. This documentation must include the following:

- An explanation of the scope of service management (to be specified in more detail in GR 3).

- A service management policy (as already described in GR 1).
- A basic service management plan and associated plans (detailed in GR 4).

Thus, this requirement can be seen as a summary of the three individual requirements listed. These components of the service management system documentation are described in the capability levels which are differentiated below (more details on the capability levels of FitSM can be found in Section 1.3 FitSM as a lightweight approach).

Capability level	Description
1	Some initial service management-related documentation is available, while key documents, like the service management scope statement, an overall service management policy or a service management plan are missing.
2	Most documents required for the implementation of an SMS are available, including a service management scope statement, an overall service management policy and a service management plan. However, not all key documents are elaborated enough to make them fully effective, e.g. the service management plan is still high-level and does not address details relevant for its implementation.
3	A clear scope statement, a service management policy and a full-service management plan have been documented in a consistent and comprehensive way, and in a sufficient level of detail to effectively support the planning and implementation of an SMS.

3.2.2 Create process descriptions

In addition to the description of the service management system, a description of the processes is necessary. These must be created and maintained. Each of these descriptions must contain or reference at least the following elements:

- Description of the process goals;
- Description of the inputs, outputs and activities of the process;
- Description of the process-specific roles and responsibilities;
- Description of the interfaces to other processes in each case;
- Related, process-specific guidelines (if appropriate);
- Related, process- or activity-specific detailed descriptions (if necessary).

The fulfillment of this requirement is complex in practice. FitSM-2 can be used as a basis for process objectives, inputs and outputs, and the activities of the processes. Many of the required contents can be found there in a simple form. For the process-specific roles and responsibilities, FitSM-3 can be used. However, it is important to extend or adapt the FitSM proposals to suit the individual company. It is of enormous benefit to deal with and reflect on the statements in FitSM-2 and FitSM-3 alone. It is only through this work that one can achieve a higher level of capability for this requirement.

Capability level	Description
1	A minority of service management processes have been defined, most documentation is very initial and does not address process goals, inputs, activities, outputs, roles and interfaces in a comprehensive way.
2	Core service management processes, in particular those having to cope with high volumes of occurrences, have been documented. Process definitions cover goals, inputs, activities, outputs, roles and interfaces in a level of detail sufficient to effectively support reliable process execution.
3	All service management processes have been documented. Every process definition covers goals, inputs, activities, outputs, roles and interfaces in the context of the respective process. Where required, process-specific policies, such as a release policy (in the context of the release and deployment management process) or information security policies (in the context of the Information Security Management process) are defined and documented. Also, for core process activities, procedures have been defined and documented, such as a procedure for performing SLA reviews, a procedure for dealing with major incidents or a procedure for assessing/approving changes.

3.2.3 Document process results

The results of activities in all service management processes must be documented and the execution of essential activities of the processes must be recorded.

FitSM requires the documentation of processes in this context. FitSM understands a document to be a piece of information (or several pieces of information), including the underlying carrier medium. Examples of documents are policies, plans, process descriptions, or even procedures. They are subject to the document governance required in GR 2.4. It is therefore advisable to create a template for documents at an early stage of planning that meets the requirements of document control. The example documents from FitSM-4 provide good ideas for this.

In addition to documentation, GR 2.3 also requires records that confirm key activities have actually been performed. A record can be:

- The documentation for an event: "A hard disk in a server has failed."
- Documenting the results of executing a process: "The change was properly implemented, documented, and completed."
- Documenting an activity: "The regular customer report on the availability of a service has been created and filed in the designated location."

These records are generated continually and are often available in large numbers. The appropriate level of detail for these records and how they are handled is defined in the corresponding process. For example, the Incident & Service Request Management process defines how records of incidents (malfunctions) are to be made. Each individual incident ticket is then a record. FitSM-6 describes each capability level this way.

Capability level	Description
1	Some outputs of service management processes are documented, but not in a consistent and repeatable way. Records of key activities performed, such as incident and change records, do not generally follow a defined format and vary in level of detail.
2	For the majority of service management processes, in particular those having to cope with high volumes of occurrences, outputs are reliably documented, and key activities are recorded in a consistent format and level of detail.
3	Outputs from all service management processes are documented in a defined and reliable way. For all key activities, records are created in defined formats and maintained in defined locations.

3.2.4 Management of documentation

Quality management systems, and thus FitSM, require that documentation be managed with the following activities in mind:

- Creation and approval;
- Communication and distribution;
- Review;
- Versioning and tracking of changes.

This requirement, therefore, regulates formal aspects related to documentation. Among other things, it ensures traceability of the activities surrounding the documentation. The capability levels are as follows.

Capability level	Description
1	It is understood that documents should be controlled, i.e. approved before they are distributed, stored at defined locations, and reviewed from time to time. However, responsibilities are not always completely clear, e.g. it is not always apparent whose task it is to review a specific document or who is authorized to approve a revision. Document control data – e.g. document owner, version, review date – is sometimes documented, sometimes not.
2	While not completely documented, responsibilities for the approval, distribution and review of almost all documents are clear, and the respective individuals perform their tasks in a repeatable way. Core service management documents, such as policies and process definitions, are stored at defined and well-known locations and are regularly reviewed, even if not always within planned intervals. Document control data (document owner, version, review date etc.) is recorded in a consistent manner for all types of service management documents but may be updated somewhat irregularly.
3	For each document, responsibilities (such as "owner") are defined and documented. Everybody involved is aware of the mechanisms for approval of documents. Communication and distribution follow a clear and consistent approach. Review intervals for different types of documents have been defined and adhered to. Document control data for all types of service management documents is recorded in sufficient detail and kept up-to-date to support effective document control. Changes to documents are traceable.

3.3 SCOPE AND STAKEHOLDERS OF SERVICE MANAGEMENT

A service management system does not necessarily have to cover the entire area of responsibility of an IT department or IT service provider. It is perfectly legitimate, and often sensible, to limit it. Typical limitations of the scope of application include:

- Services:
  "Only those services that support the customer's core processes are provided according to defined specifications. For other services, improvisation is more in demand."
- Customers:
  "As a supplier in the automotive industry, a company must demonstrate to the car manufacturer that a functioning SMS exists in all areas relevant to the car manufacturer."
- Locations:
  "Processes that are applied in a specific data center or at a location should have a defined level of quality."

There are many factors to take into consideration when defining the appropriate scope for the service management system. A narrower definition offers the possibility of gaining experience in the first step and then extending it to a larger scope. However, it may also be easier not to define the scope too narrowly, as processes would otherwise have to be unnecessarily restricted. For example, it must be decided on a case-by-case basis whether it is practicable to limit incident handling by the Incident & Service Request Management process to a single site, individual services, or only specific customers.

The scope can also extend beyond the area of responsibility of a single service provider. This is supported by FitSM through the federated approach, in which several service providers form a federation, i.e., an association (see Chapter 10 Federated IT infrastructures).

The relevant scope is largely determined by the requirements of the stakeholders. After all, we do not operate a service management system as an end in itself. Typical stakeholders are management, employees, customers and suppliers. However, the legislator can also be a stakeholder group, e.g. if there are requirements for proof or deletion periods in certain areas.

The scope of the service management system is derived from this. FitSM formulates two requirements for this:

- GR 3.1: Identify stakeholder expectations;
- GR 3.2: Define the scope of the SMS.

GR 3.1: Identify stakeholder expectations
As part of a stakeholder analysis, all interest groups (stakeholders) in the scope must be identified. Needs and expectations are analyzed for each stakeholder group, especially if these are contractually agreed or legal requirements exist.

Capability level	Description
1	Information on stakeholders and the legal and contractual context of the organization is only partially documented. Documentation is scattered throughout the organization. Most relevant information, even if not documented, is known to someone in the organization, but it is not always obvious who the right contact person is.
2	Information on stakeholders and the legal and contractual context of the organization is sufficiently documented. Documentation is scattered across various sources. However, competent contacts who maintain these sources are known to most internal parties, or can at least be quickly identified.
3	Information on stakeholders, their interests and expectations, as well as the legal and contractual context of the organization is documented. There is a defined place where this information is collected, or at least linked to.

GR 3.2: Define the scope of the SMS

The requirements of the relevant stakeholders are taken into account when defining the scope. Furthermore, it is described so clearly that there is no room for interpretation about the boundaries.

Capability level	Description
1	There is a common understanding of what scope the SMS should have, but this is largely undocumented.
2	There is a general scope statement or statements on scope exist in service management documents, e.g. within policy or process definitions, which are not necessarily aligned with each other and may or may not be approved by top management.
3	A comprehensive scope statement exists that describes the scope of the SMS taking into account physical locations, affected services, customers, infrastructure(s), technology and any other relevant parameters that might limit or broaden the scope. The scope statement is based on the stakeholder analysis, has been approved and communicated to relevant parties by the service provider's top management.

3.4 CONTINUAL IMPROVEMENT (PLAN-DO-CHECK-ACT)

The PDCA cycle (also known as the Deming cycle after its author William Edwards Deming) has become an integral part of quality assurance in recent decades. It is the basis of the ISO 9000 quality management standard and the continual improvement process. Agile frameworks and methods also use this procedure.

FitSM uses this approach and has formulated four areas in the general requirements. The aim is to plan the scope, level of detail and requirements for an SMS, implement them, measure the degree of target achievement and identify opportunities for improvement.

In each pass, the targets can be raised further until the desired level is reached. After that, further optimization or simply the maintenance of the status quo can be pursued. In this way, the PDCA cycle can be used to bring the entire SMS with all its processes to the desired level of maturity. It represents a continual improvement process, i.e.

the endeavor to constantly and at short intervals search for the causes of errors to permanently improve the services, processes and organization instead of working with larger-scale programs.

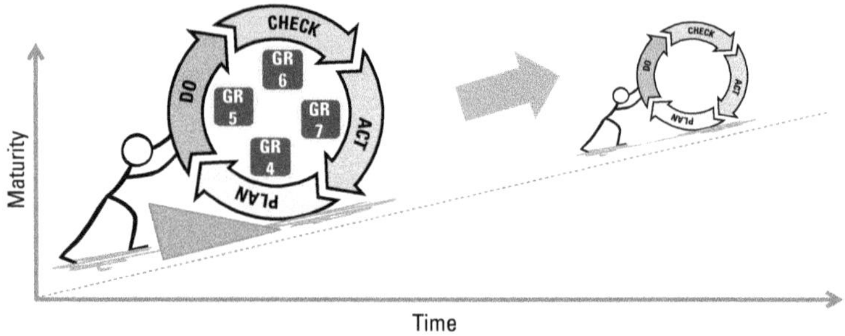

Figure 7: Increasing the maturity level via the PDCA cycle

In the planning phase (PLAN), quality improvement measures are developed, followed by implementation and testing in the next phase (DO). It is important to act in shorter cycles and to select simple measures that can be implemented quickly. The CHECK phase is then used to review and evaluate the effectiveness of the measures. In the last phase (ACT), sources of error are eliminated and corrective measures are initiated. At the end, the leap back to the first phase takes place, resulting in a continual, sustainable improvement. Important here is quality assurance, which is intended to prevent a slide back into worse (original) states. In Figure 7 this is shown as a wedge under the cycle wheel.

This cycle can also be found in agile process models, where fast feedback is desired and demanded. The PDCA cycle has been implemented in the general requirements GR 4 to GR 7.

- PLAN: Service management planning (GR 4);
- DO: Implementation of service management (GR 5);
- CHECK: Monitor and review service management (GR 6);
- ACT: Continual Improvement of service management (GR 7).

3.4.1 Service management planning

FitSM calls for planning that includes the overarching roles, responsibilities, required training and awareness, and tools needed to support the SMS. The objective of this phase in FitSM is therefore to create a plan for the introduction and maintenance of service management for a service provider. This must be based on an identified scope according to GR 3.

At this stage, it is important to define targets and performance indicators for this. In practice, those responsible must think about how they want to measure the achievement of what is planned in each case. To this end, the corresponding actual status must also be documented in order to make the change transparent and recognizable at a later date.

Ideally, the goals should be specified by top management, thus aligning the activities in IT service management with the business. Finding suitable performance indicators is not an easy task. It has proven effective to start with a few values and to pay attention to the achievability of the targets. By starting with a smaller number of metrics, organizations can prevent unnecessary frustration, or the impression that targets are unreasonable or unachievable.

These activities must be carried out:

- Assessment of the current maturity level of the service management system.
- Definition of an appropriate target of a maturity level to be achieved for service management (qualitative or quantitative).
- Identification and description of the discrepancy between defined target and current assessment.
- Identification and specification of activities for improvement based on the discrepancy.
- Creation of a service management plan that should include, but not be limited to, the following topics:
  - Definition of the goals and a time schedule for the implementation of the service management system and the necessary processes;
  - Definition and assignment of basic roles and responsibilities in the service management system;
  - Definition and assignment of roles and responsibilities for the processes;
  - Creation of a schedule for selected tasks;
  - Clarification of the tools to be used for supporting the implementation of the service management system and for the operational execution of the processes.

The following two requirements must be fulfilled for the planning

- GR 4.1: Create and maintain service management plan;
- GR 4.2: Align all plans.

GR 4.1: Create and maintain service management plan

The above-mentioned activities of this phase result in a plan. Among other things, this plan regulates responsibilities for the individual tasks in the following phases. Furthermore, it is subordinate to other plans that cover individual tasks. For example, this higher-level plan can coordinate the planning of individual process implementations and plan the interfaces between the processes.

The specific contents of the service management plan are described in this requirement. The plan must contain the following elements or at least refer to separate documentation:

- Objectives and timing of the implementation of the SMS and related processes;
- Overarching roles and responsibilities;
- Training and awareness activities required;
- Required technology (tools / techniques) to support the SMS.

Capability level	Description
1	The service provider is aware that IT service management needs to be planned. However, it is not clear who is accountable and responsible for service management planning. Plans on specific topics might exist but are not well aligned to each other.
2	There is a generally good understanding of the responsibilities around service management planning activities, i.e. who is responsible for which part of the overall plan, and who is accountable for service management planning as a whole. These responsibilities are not consistently documented, and in some instances, there might be some confusion regarding the distribution of responsibilities. The practices for creating and maintaining specific plans, e.g. the plans for implementing individual service management processes, are not entirely consistent and plans may vary in terms of their structure and level of detail.
3	IT service management is planned and the roles and responsibilities related to planning activities are clearly defined and documented. A consistent and documented approach is used to create and maintain plans. Plans are created using common templates and have a similar, appropriate level of detail. The service management plan addresses the objectives and timeline for implementing service management processes, roles and responsibilities, training and awareness-raising activities, and the necessary supporting technology (tools).

GR 4.2: Align all plans

Each process-specific plan must be aligned with the overall service management plan. The higher-level service management plan has a coordinating function here.

The more people who take on the roles of SMS owner and process owner, the greater the need for coordination. Without such coordination, conflicting goals can arise. This results in people sabotaging each other, consciously or unconsciously.

For this purpose, the capability levels are formulated as follows.

Capability level	Description
1	Process-specific plans are developed largely independently. Not too much attention is paid to ensuring that they are consistent with the overall service management plan. When inconsistencies emerge, they are discussed and resolved on a case-by-case basis.
2	Process managers are aware of the need to align processes with each other and with the overall SMS. Care is taken to ensure that process-specific plans are aligned with the overall service management plan. Regular activities in the preparation of process-specific plans include coordination meetings with other process managers.
3	The alignment of process-specific plans with each other and with the overall service management plan is a key element of a structured and defined approach to the development of process-specific plans and projects.

3.4.2 Implementation of service management

The second phase of the PDCA cycle involves the 'DO'. Specifically, the service management system and processes are then established and practically implemented according to the schedule defined in the previous phase. If you have clarified the scope in GR 3 and have agreed on smaller steps for implementation, this phase should proceed in a manageable time frame. The following requirements should be considered:

- GR 5.1: Implement the service management plan;
- GR 5.2: Apply process practices.

GR 5.1: Implement the service management plan

Depending on the scope and level of detail of the service management plan, this means, among other things, describing the processes, training employees and new role owners, and coordinating the process interfaces.

Capability level	Description
1	There is a general understanding of the need to implement IT service management processes and related activities according to plans. However, sometimes practical implementation does not follow plans.
2	The service management plan is implemented, and the persons involved are aware of their specific duties in implementing parts of the plan.
3	The service management plan is implemented according to defined and assigned responsibilities. The activities carried out are recorded to ensure they are retraceable.

GR 5.2: Apply process practices

Within the scope of the SMS, the defined service management processes must be followed and their practical application enforced, as well as compliance with associated policies and procedures. It should be clear how non-compliance is identified and handled.

Capability level	Description
1	Not all staff members are aware of the necessity to adhere to policies, processes and procedures. Processes are frequently bypassed. Process managers react to this in various, not always consistent ways.
2	Service management processes are largely followed in practice, and people involved comply with related policies and procedures. Where process managers discover that their processes are bypassed or procedures not adhered to, they react in a consistent way and escalate hierarchically where necessary.
3	With very few exceptions, service management policies, processes and procedures are followed in practice. SMS owner, SMS manager, process owners and process managers are committed to ensuring a high level of adherence. Reactions to repeated non-adherence are defined and include, as a last resort after multiple instances of intentional non-compliance, disciplinary actions.

3.4.3 Monitor and review the service management system

After the activities from the 'DO' phase have been established, visible and measurable results should become apparent. In the 'CHECK' phase, these are checked for the achievement of objectives (effectiveness) and the appropriate use of resources (efficiency). How exactly one can proceed here is explained in more detail later. FitSM formulates two requirements for this area:

- GR 6.1: Measure effectiveness of the service management system;
- GR 6.2: Determine SMS maturity level regularly.

GR 6.1: Measure effectiveness of the service management system

The effectiveness and performance of the SMS and its service management processes must be measured and evaluated using appropriate performance indicators to determine the extent to which defined or agreed objectives are being achieved (see Section 3.4.1 Service management planning).

Capability level	Description
1	The service provider is aware that measurements are important to support continual improvement of service delivery and IT service management. While some activities to measure and review the effectiveness of IT service management processes may be carried out from time to time, they do not follow a structured and generally well-understood approach.
2	To understand if IT service management processes are effective, key performance indicators (metrics) are measured and reported for most processes on a regular basis.
3	For all IT service management processes, meaningful key performance indicators have been defined and are measured and reported according to defined plans and schedules. Performance indicators are specific, measurable, achievable, relevant and time-framed (SMART) and help identify potential improvements to processes or the SMS as a whole. They are based on clearly defined goals and critical success factors.

GR 6.2: Determine SMS maturity level regularly

To establish continual improvement in the sense of the PDCA cycle, assessments and/or audits of the SMS are to be carried out. In this process, the identified performance indicators are reviewed and checked against target values. The degree of maturity and the level of conformity are determined to check the success of the activities to date.

Capability level	Description
1	The service provider is aware that assessments and reviews/audits are important to support continual improvement of service delivery and IT service management. However, reviews or audits often do not follow a clearly scheduled and structured approach. Maturity assessments, if any, are limited to some self-assessments from time to time.
2	To identify nonconformities, i.e. situations in which defined processes are bypassed or not correctly executed, reviews and audits of IT service management processes and the SMS as a whole are conducted on a regular basis. These may include internal and external audits. The overall maturity of the SMS is evaluated at regular intervals.
3	A scheduled program for reviews, audits and maturity assessments is in place, and activities are carried out according to this program. Reviews and audits are conducted according to clearly defined guidelines or procedures. For each audit, a detailed audit plan is created reflecting the audit criteria. The results of reviews, audits and assessments are recorded in a structured and uniform manner and reported to relevant stakeholders. Each audit report covers the findings and conclusions drawn from the audit in a structured way. Follow-up audits are planned under consideration of the results from previous audits.

3.4.4 Continual improvement of service management

In the 'ACT' phase, the results from the measurements are evaluated and opportunities for improvement are identified. According to effort and potential benefit, they can be prioritized and implemented, or discarded. Here, two requirements are formulated:

- GR 7.1: Identify and correct target deviations;
- GR 7.2: Plan and implement improvements.

GR 7.1: Identify and correct target deviations

Non-conformities and deviations from defined and agreed targets must be identified and corrective action initiated to prevent recurrence. At this point, the character of incremental improvement clearly comes into play. Meaningful reviews and manageable measures make it possible to correct identified deviations quickly and easily. The capability levels for this are as follows:

Capability level	Description
1	The service provider is aware that deviations from intended outcomes and nonconformities should be identified and corrective action taken, and some actions towards this are generally taken. However, a structured approach is missing.
2	Nonconformities and deviations from intended outcomes are detected by unscheduled, but regular reviews of reports on key performance indicators, assessments and audits. Identification of deviations and nonconformities consistently trigger corrective actions. However, neither the results of these actions nor the overall approach are always sufficiently documented.
3	Nonconformities and deviations from targets are detected by scheduled reviews of reports on key performance indicators, assessments and audits. Identified nonconformities and deviations are recorded and follow-up actions triggered and documented. Roles and responsibilities in this context are clearly defined.

GR 7.2: Plan and implement improvements

Identified opportunities for improvement are planned and implemented in accordance with the Continual Service Improvement Management process. From the PDCA cycle for establishing or further developing the service management system, activities are transferred directly to the operational process.

Capability level	Description
1	The service provider is aware that continual improvement must be actively promoted throughout the organization. However, the roles and activities to plan and implement improvements are undefined, and improvements are handled on a case-by-case basis.
2	Improvements to the SMS are managed according to well-understood responsibilities. For example, every manager and owner are aware of their duties in identifying and managing improvements to the process or service under their responsibility.
3	Responsibilities in the context of identifying, managing and reviewing the success of improvements are clearly defined as part of the Continual Service Improvement Management process. This process is consistently followed for improving the service management policy, the service management plan and all service management processes.

4 Offer and Agree

In the realm of service provision, envisioning it as a business transaction where customers receive tailored services is key. Understanding both existing and potential customers, as well as your own suite of services, forms the foundation. Customers require a designated point of contact within the IT service provider—a conduit for conveying new requirements, troubleshooting, expressing preferences, and posing inquiries to their service provider. Simultaneously, it's imperative to meticulously develop, articulate, and contractually define your services. Establishing and maintaining robust communication channels with customers further enriches this dynamic relationship.

In practice, the question is often encountered as to the order in which the processes of the ITSM framework should be utilized. FitSM makes a point of clarifying fundamental questions (top management responsibility or scope of the service management system) before answering this question and, if necessary, including them in the service management plan. These are described in the previous chapter "General requirements". From a business perspective, the first step should be to take care of the entry into the value chain of the IT service provider. It is important to develop IT service provider services and make them customer-oriented, to bring them closer to the recipients and, finally, to create transparency in terms of the costs. These tasks are assigned to the following processes in FitSM:

- Customer Relationship Management (CRM);
- Service Portfolio Management (SPM);
- Service Level Management (SLM).

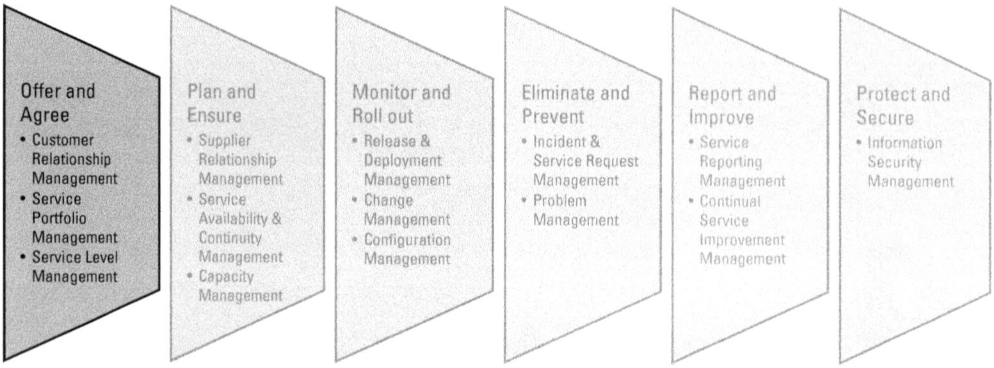

Figure 8: FitSM process model for Offer and Agree

4.1 CUSTOMER RELATIONSHIP MANAGEMENT

The Customer Relationship Management process describes the tasks involved in establishing and maintaining a good relationship with customers who receive the services. In practice, this process is often not viewed with due appreciation. Service providers and their employees are often well organized as far as the fulfillment of their operational tasks is concerned and know their duties. However, they forget, for example, to communicate with the customer, whether this is about their offers or the handling of feedback (FitSM uses the term 'complaints'). It is therefore important to organize effective customer relationship on the service providers' side.

4.1.1 Process description

The term 'customer' within the realm of IT service management, refers to an organization or a specific unit within an organization that collaborates with a service provider for the delivery of one or more services. In its simplest form, this relationship may involve the customer receiving IT services, with IT acting without explicitly receiving orders. It's crucial to differentiate between users, who directly benefit from and utilize a service, and customers. This distinction is vital as both groups have distinct requirements, leading to varied interfaces with the service provider.

When a customer has specific requirements, they typically engage with a customer relationship manager or account manager. On the other hand, users interact with the Service Desk, reporting issues and making service requests, a process encompassed within the Incident & Service Request Management process. Depending on the nature of the inquiry, an individual can approach the service provider both as a customer and as a user. It's important to note that the term 'customer' is conceptualized broadly in FitSM, often representing a collective set of users.

Depending on the type of service provider, customers may be external (a legally independent service provider) or internal (in the case of an IT department). Regardless of this, these customers must be identified. When identifying internal customers, the question often arises as to the levels at which services are to be offered and commissioned. If services affect the entire organization equally, the management is usually the appropriate contact. For services with a departmental focus, department heads are more likely to be considered as representatives of middle management. However, team leaders or project managers can also be potential customers and thus contacts.

Each customer is assigned an account manager who familiarizes themself with the customer and their specific requirements, acts as the contact person for feedback, and keeps an eye on customer satisfaction. This may be the same person who draws up the agreements with the customer through an SLA as part of the Service Portfolio Management process. This person must be very easy for the customer to reach. The customer must know how to contact their account manager.

The account manager regularly conducts a service review with the customers they support, i.e., a review of the services booked by the respective customer. This involves evaluating the service provided and its quality. This can be done in dialog with the customer, or on the basis of customer feedback. The result of a service review serves as the basis for identifying potential for improvement, from which follow-up measures can be derived if necessary. A service review is therefore a tool for controlling the value of a service, i.e. the benefit generated from a service by a customer and the associated users.

In the Customer Relationship Management process, it is necessary to regulate how the customer's requirements and feedback are recorded and how customer satisfaction can be measured. Only in this way can a uniform, comparable result be achieved, even in the case of several customer service representatives, and it can be ensured that the desired quality is achieved in dealing with customers, their requirements and implementation. For this purpose, the activities are documented in a customer database, which must be set up when the process is initialized.

The following graphic depicts the activities for initializing the Customer Relationship Management process, which are then transformed into regular activities.

4.1.2 Roles in the process

The **process owner** assumes overall responsibility for the process and in doing so should promote a functioning interface with the Service Portfolio Management process.

For the **process manager** appointed by the process owner, the main operational tasks in this process are as follows:

- Maintenance of the customer database.
- Ensuring that customers' feedback is handled in a process-compliant manner.
- Coordination of the determination of customer satisfaction.
- Review of the results of service evaluations with customers.

Figure 9: Activities in the Customer Relationship Management process

There is an **account manager** for each customer. He or she serves as the primary contact person for the respective customers and maintains the relationship with them through regular communication. They also take up feedback and conduct service reviews together with customers. From the perspective of the process, they are the case owner for the customer.

4.1.3 Requirements

For the practical implementation of the process, FitSM establishes the following six requirements:

- CRM 7.1: Identify service customers;
- CRM 7.2: Establish contact points for customers;
- CRM 7.3: Establish communication channels for customers;
- CRM 7.4: Conduct service reviews regularly;
- CRM 7.5: Handle customer feedback in a uniform manner;
- CRM 7.6: Manage customer satisfaction.

CRM 7.1: Identify service customers

For the provision of services, the service provider must identify the respective customers and record this in writing. The result must be documented and kept up-to-date, as well as being standardized and stored in a system. The associated capability levels are described in FitSM-6 as follows:

Capability level	Description
1	Customers are internally known. There are customer lists, but these are updated irregularly and may not be comprehensive and accurate.
2	There is a list or several lists, containing information of all service customers. The lists are maintained on an informal basis, but without clear responsibilities for doing so. Lists are not aligned to each other and may contain redundant information, have different formats, contain a different level of detail and redundant information.
3	There is a list of all customers, with its maintenance based on documented responsibilities.

CRM 7.2: Establish contact points for customers

For each customer, there must be a designated contact person who is responsible for shaping and managing the customer relationship as well as customer satisfaction. This aspect has already been described in the previous section (customer service representatives). Of course, a contact person can also be responsible for managing multiple customers, i.e., be responsible for a group. The following capability levels are defined by FitSM-6:

Capability level	Description
1	There is no designated contact for each customer, but individuals from the service provider have a basic understanding of the need to manage customer relationships.
2	There is a person or role generally assigned to each specific customer or group of customers. This assignment is not necessarily based on documented responsibilities and management of the relationship with the customer and their satisfaction may be inconsistent.
3	There is a person or role assigned to each specific customer or group of customers that manages the relationship and satisfaction based on documented responsibilities.

CRM 7.3: Establish communication channels for customers

Furthermore, communication with customers must be regulated. This rather general formulation can be developed differently in practice. Since the Customer Relationship Management process tends to be aimed more overridingly at a good relationship with customers, personal contact is generally the most important instrument. Events in the sense of an in-house exhibition or specialist conference can also be used. Of course, webinars or other online live events can also be organized. An information portal for customers or users, the publication of details on how incidents have been resolved, or a regular newsletter are also conceivable. A communication plan should be drawn up to document communication channels, content, frequency and contact persons. The following capability levels can then be differentiated in detail:

Capability level	Description
1	Communication with customers is possible but occurs in a haphazard way and on demand. There is no single clear list of customer communication channels, and it may prove difficult to communicate with customers in a timely manner.
2	There are established communication channels for each customer or group of customers, but it is tied to the individual or role assigned to it. The communication channels, including mechanisms for service ordering, escalation and complaint, are recorded in some centralized location but not in a consistent way.
3	Communication channels for each customer or group of customers, including mechanisms for service ordering, escalation and complaint, are recorded in a single, consistent way based on documented responsibilities.

CRM 7.4: Conduct service reviews regularly

This requirement allows the customer to participate in the evaluation of the service quality. These reviews serve to further develop the scope and the topics of the service, if necessary, also to reduce or expand the subject matter. If there is little scope for contract design, the reviews serve to permanently monitor performance and improve the agreed quality of the services. It is important that these reviews are carried out regularly and in conjunction with the customer.

Capability level	Description
1	Informal service reviews occur, based on interactions between customer representatives and the provider. These occur on demand, following major problems or are somewhat randomly based on the individuals involved.
2	Service reviews occur regularly but remain inconsistent and dependent on the individuals performing them, whilst responsibilities are not clearly documented. Review procedures and records may be kept but not in a systematic way.
3	Service reviews are carried out at planned intervals, as well as on demand and following major issues. Reviews are based on defined responsibilities and generate systematic records of the review.

CRM 7.5: Handle customer feedback in a uniform manner

The handling of customer feedback regarding services must also be organized. To this end, every customer must have the opportunity to complain easily and at the appropriate contact point. The management of customer feedback should be seen as an important opportunity for the service provider to derive suggestions for improvement from the feedback of its customers (i.e., from a specific situation and/or dissatisfaction). The term 'customer satisfaction' includes user satisfaction. In some instances, service providers may fail to effectively communicate agreed-upon service targets to their customers. As a result, users may develop unrealistic expectations, leading to misaligned satisfaction levels. Typically, a record-based satisfaction survey is conducted among users to assess service quality. However, in some instances, the survey results reveal a discrepancy between user expectations and the agreed-upon service levels or contractual terms. The following capability levels are distinguished in FitSM-6:

Capability level	Description
1	Customer complaints are managed on a case-by-case basis, generally by the individual receiving them or a colleague who they pass it on to. There is no formal record of the complaint.
2	Customer complaints are managed and records of the complaints are created and maintained, though these may not be consistent. Responsibility is not documented but there is a general understanding of who should manage complaints.
3	Customer complaints are managed based on documented responsibilities, generating consistent records.

CRM 7.6: Manage customer satisfaction

The wording of this requirement in FitSM is somewhat unfortunate. Customer satisfaction must be worked on continually instead of just being "managed". However, this requirement is important. It focuses on the satisfaction of the service provider's customers. In this respect, this requirement describes all activities that are necessary to ensure a satisfied customer. Customers should be asked, for example, at which points they are satisfied with the service, and satisfaction should be made measurable in concrete terms. In addition, a procedure should be established that is as objective as possible for surveying customer satisfaction. Questions in a service review such as "How satisfied were you with our service performance in the month?" are too general. Furthermore, if possible, the same group of people should always be asked about satisfaction so that continuity is achieved.

Specifically, the following capability levels are formulated:

Capability level	Description
1	Customer satisfaction is collected through informal means, when there is a need (such as customer demand, a complaint or a change to the service).
2	There are mechanisms for measuring customer satisfaction, which are used by the provider. However, they are used in an irregular manner and responsibility for their use is not documented.
3	Mechanisms that measure customer satisfaction are used at regular intervals based on documented responsibilities. Records of results are kept in a consistent way.

4.2 SERVICE PORTFOLIO MANAGEMENT

The purpose of this process is to maintain the service portfolio and to manage services through their lifecycle, which is often deemed crucial for fostering collaboration with customers. It serves to heighten the service provider's awareness of its offerings and the initiation of service orientation, as well as recognizing what it lacks in its portfolio. This awareness empowers the IT service provider to decline offerings if they cannot fulfill customer requirements based on their current offerings. Notably, the provider isn't obligated to fulfill every user demand, especially if it's not economically viable. When executed effectively, this process enables the service provider to strategize and proactively mold its service offerings.

4.2.1 Process description

The service portfolio is an internal list that contains information about all services that are planned, being offered or have been retired by the service provider. They are listed in the portfolio during development and remain in it even when they are taken out of service. This makes it possible to determine at any time which services are planned, which are currently available, or which are no longer available.

When it has been determined through the Service Portfolio Management process that a service is ready to be offered to customers for ordering, the description of the service and selected content should be published in the service catalog. A customer can book services based on the service catalog. While the service portfolio represents the internal view, the service catalog is the external representation.

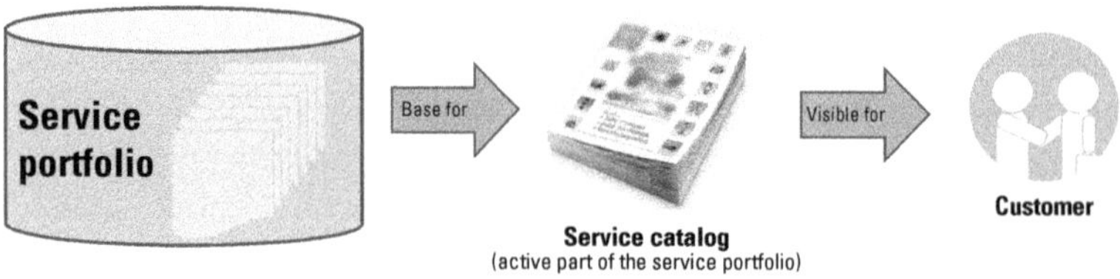

Figure 10: From the service portfolio to the customer

When a service is no longer actively offered, it can also be marked accordingly (e.g. 'retired' or 'decommissioned') or archived which means it should no longer appear in the service catalog. Sometimes, however, services that have been taken out of service should still be available temporarily. For example, it may be necessary to access data from the last ten years during a tax audit. Therefore, even when a service is decommissioned, it should be checked whether it should nevertheless continue to be part of the service portfolio, even if it is no longer made available in regular operation, i.e., is no longer actively used.

A Service Design & Transition Package (SDTP) is intended to contain the most important information about a service and should be created as early as possible. It represents the entirety of all planning for the design and transition of a specific new or modified service. It does not have to be a single document. Rather, it can be understood as an umbrella term for many documented plans and other relevant information that may be available in different formats.

A Service Design & Transition Package should specifically include the following aspects:
- Service requirements;
- Service acceptance criteria;
- Project planning;
- Communication and training plan;
- Technical plans and specifications;
- Resource plans;
- Schedules for development and go-live.

The Service Design & Transition Package contains, among other things, the service acceptance criteria (SAC). These are the criteria that must be met before a service is made available to customers and users. They are defined when a service is designed or modified. They are often updated or refined during the development phase of a service. They can cover functional and/or non-functional aspects of the specific service to be rolled out.

The task of the Service Portfolio Management process is to build up a service portfolio, define which aspects of services are to be documented in it, and keep the service portfolio constantly up-to-date. The procedure for planning new or changed services must be defined and the definition of a Service Design & Transition Package with all its associated components must be created. In addition, the organization that supports the service delivery must be identified. Often this is the entire service provider. However, it may be that only part of the organization is involved in service delivery, or several service providers may be delivering a service together as a federation. The scope of the organizational structure is strongly determined by the choice of the scope of the SMS.

The requirement that services should also be included in planning, and that all necessary information be found in this overview, makes it clear that this process takes account of the strategic planning aspects. It must be clarified as early as possible who will ensure operation (if necessary, also with the involvement of external suppliers) and what the financial view of this new IT service will be.

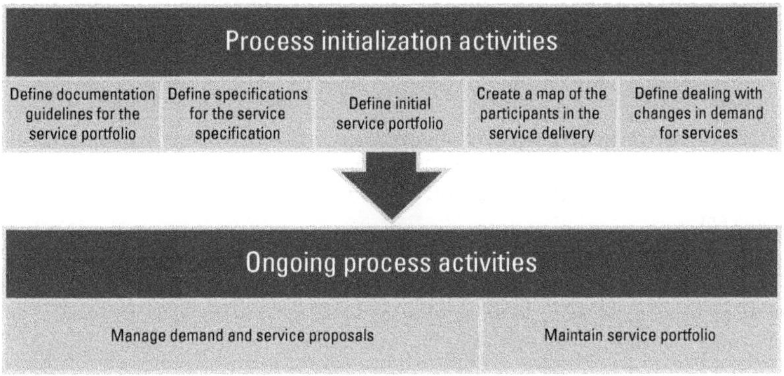

Figure 11: Activities in the Service Portfolio Management process

4.2.2 Roles in the process

In addition to assuming overall responsibility for the process and defining the objectives, the **process owner** in Service Portfolio Management should take a close look at the interfaces with Service Portfolio Management and Change Management. Both of these processes are required when a service or service component is transferred to the production environment and thus published to the service catalog.

The operational tasks of the process manager include the following activities in particular:

- Maintain the service portfolio, including management of updates to the service portfolio.
- Perform a regular review of the service portfolio.
- Ensure that the planning and development of new or changed services are in line with the Service Portfolio Management process.
- Make sure that Service Design & Transition Packages are created and managed.

Beyond that, FitSM does not define any other roles in Service Portfolio Management. This process is the only one that does not specify a case owner.

4.2.3 Requirements

Four requirements are formulated for the Service Portfolio Management process:

- SPM 1.1: Specify and maintain service portfolio;
- SPM 1.2: Evaluate service proposals;
- SPM 1.3: Plan design and transition for services;
- SPM 1.4: Identify organizational support.

SPM 1.1: Specify and maintain service portfolio

A well-maintained service portfolio forms a basis for the structured planning of IT services. In addition to technical considerations, a service portfolio also addresses strategic and, thus, business-relevant aspects. Meeting this requirement ensures that the IT service provider develops its service in a structured manner and with appropriate longer-term planning. In FitSM-6, the following capability levels are described for this purpose:

Capability level	Description
1	The organization is generally aware of what services it offers, and can describe them and any related information in some undefined format. However, the 'services' may be closer to components than to value-generating services as considered by IT service management.
2	There is a communal understanding of the service offerings, including past, current and planned services. A list of service specifications is maintained on an informal basis. The specified services are services as seen by IT service management, each individually generating identifiable value for customers.
3	There is a defined procedure for maintaining the service portfolio with clearly documented responsibilities. The portfolio lists all services as well as useful information related to their technical components, dependencies, service management, value generations and business case. This is shared across the organization.

SPM 1.2: Evaluate service proposals

The process of designing and transitioning new services or modifications to existing ones requires careful planning and evaluation. This planning ensures that the long-term success of IT services is factored in, even when changes are made. The evaluation should consider anticipated demand, necessary resources, and expected benefits. Regardless of the outcome, the insights gained from this assessment are valuable. Depending on the nature of the changes, they can be managed as either a straightforward change or a more complex project during operational implementation. The capability levels are defined as follows:

Capability level	Description
1	Proposals for new or changed services are managed on an ad-hoc basis, without a standard approach or control. The considerations of predicted demand, required resources and expected benefits depend on the individual efforts. Plans for services are delivered inconsistently and in varying forms and formats.
2	There is an understanding of the need for a structured approach for the transition to new or changed services, together with consideration of predicted demand, required resources and expected benefits in the proposals. The implementation is inconsistent and varies in form and format.

Capability level	Description
3	There is a clear, documented and established approach to handling new or changed services, that considers predicted demand, required resources and expected benefits in the proposals.

SPM 1.3: Plan design and transition for services

This requirement emphasizes the importance of effectively managing the evolution of services throughout their lifecycle. It focuses on the need to carefully plan the introduction of new services as well as significant changes to existing services. The planning process should consider various factors such as timescales, assigning responsibilities, incorporating new or updated technologies, establishing effective communication channels, and defining criteria for the acceptance of the services. This underscores the significance of proactive planning and strategic decision-making. It points out that successful service management requires a holistic approach that considers the entire lifecycle of a service. This requirement enables organizations to adapt and optimize their service offerings, ultimately leading to improved customer satisfaction and business success. The capability levels for this requirement are as follows:

Capability level	Description
1	For some new or changed services, design and transition are planned and documented. The focus is primarily on the technical and functional aspects of service delivery, but timelines, responsibilities, communication and acceptance criteria are not always considered.
2	Services are controlled over most of their lifecycle, but certain transitions, e.g. towards deactivation, are not considered. For all new or changed services, design and transition are consistently planned and documented. Important aspects such as timeframes and responsibilities are considered as part of this planning, as well as functionality and necessary technical changes.
3	Services are controlled throughout their lifecycle, from initial planning to deactivation. The lifecycle phases of services are clearly defined, as are the criteria that must be met in each case for a successful transition to a new phase. These acceptance criteria are not only functional and technical but also take into account organizational and communication aspects. Transition plans have a standardized structure and reliably take into account schedules, responsibilities, technology, communication and testing of acceptance criteria.

SPM 1.4: Identify organizational support

This requirement focuses on the importance of identifying and managing the suppliers involved in delivering a service, both internally and externally. It stresses the need to establish clear communication channels and to define roles and responsibilities for each supplier. Additionally, if federation members fall within the relevant stakeholders, there is a need to identify and coordinate with them. Effectively identifying and managing service suppliers is crucial for seamless service delivery. By clearly determining the contact points, roles, and responsibilities of each supplier, organizations can establish effective lines of communication and ensure accountability throughout the service lifecycle. This approach enables organizations to streamline their supplier relationships, optimize collaboration, and enhance the overall service quality. The inclusion of federation members underscores the need to acknowledge and coordinate with external entities that can affect service delivery, fostering collaboration to achieve desired outcomes. The capability levels for this requirement are as follows:

Capability level	Description
1	There is some understanding of the structure supporting service provision, but it is mostly related to technical functions and individuals. There is little mapping to departmental, organizational or federation structure and agreement within the supporting structure is reliant on relationships between individuals.
2	There is an understanding of the arrangement of departments, organizations and federations that underlies service delivery. Members of the different groups share a common vision of the relationships between them, but it may vary in detail and is hard to control.
3	There is a well understood relationship between the internal and external groups underlying service delivery, based on agreed and documented responsibilities and supported by appropriate agreements.

4.3 SERVICE LEVEL MANAGEMENT

The objective of this process is to maintain service catalogs, and to define and evaluate agreements on service quality with customers and suppliers. This is set into operation by establishing meaningful service level agreements (SLA) and supporting operational level agreements (OLA) with internal groups and underpinning agreements (UA) with suppliers.

4.3.1 Process description

In the first step, a service catalog is created from the service portfolio, which provides the customer with an overview of all active services offered and all relevant information about these services. The service catalog thus contains the services that can be booked (commissioned) directly by the customer or user. A service catalog is updated when a service goes into operation or is retired. Relevant changes to a service must constantly be updated in the service catalog so that all information on services is meaningful for customers and users.

ITSM practice differentiates between service catalog and service request types. These are two different concepts within the realm of IT service management (ITSM). The service catalog can be described as follows and is part of the FitSM process Service Level Management:

- The service catalog is a comprehensive list of all IT services offered by an IT service provider.
- It describes the available services, their characteristics, scope, costs, service level objectives, and any other relevant information.

- The service catalog serves as a reference point for customers to understand the available services and select those that meet their requirements.
- It also helps internal teams to provide consistent information about the services offered and manage service delivery.

Service request types differ from that and are part of the Incident & Service Request Management process:
- Service request types refer to the various types of requests or tasks that customers or users can submit to the IT service provider.
- These types can cover a wide range of service requests, such as asking for access rights, provisioning new hardware or software, requesting support or assistance with issues, etc.
- Each service request type may have specific processes and workflows defined to process and fulfill the request.
- Managing service request types enables the service provider to respond efficiently to customer needs and ensure that requests are handled appropriately.

Overall, the service catalog is a structured list of available services, while service request types represent the different types of requests that can be made to the service provider. The service catalog informs customers about the service provider's offerings, while service request types organize the processing and fulfillment of customer requests in the Incident & Service Request Management process.

The customer chooses a service from the service catalog, specifying the desired performance level. Subsequently, a Service Level Agreement (SLA) is established between the customer and the service provider. SLAs may not necessarily be individually negotiated between the service provider and each customer for specific services. Instead, there can be overarching SLAs or a standardized SLA applicable to one, multiple, or all services. Hence, an SLA serves as a binding agreement delineating the specifics of service provision. Elements outlined in the service catalog can be seamlessly incorporated into the SLA with reference to the catalog. However, any additional details or modifications must be explicitly specified and mutually agreed upon.

An SLA often includes the following content:
- Description of the service and service level;
- Service targets;
- Quantity structure (e.g. number of data records, expected access numbers);
- Service and operating hours;
- Scheduled service interruptions;
- Obligations on the customer side;
- Obligations of the service provider;
- Escalation and notification procedures;
- Utilization limits;

- Information on billing (for example, service price);
- Regulations in the event of non-compliance;
- Measures to be taken in the event of incidents or disasters;
- Limited functionality for emergency operation in the event of a disaster;
- Term and termination;
- Service reporting (content, design, . . .);
- Service review cycle;
- Glossary of terms.

Which aspects play a role in a specific SLA can only be decided on a case-by-case basis. It is possible that individual points mentioned above may be omitted or that others may be added.

In addition to the service description, the service targets form an essential part of an SLA. They specify the performance level of important features, such as the availability, configuration, or equipment of a service. The definition of a service target includes a measurable target value and a clear description of how this is measured.

Since the service catalog serves as the basis for creating an SLA, the Service Portfolio Management process has the task of keeping the basic information for the service catalog constantly up-to-date.

Once an SLA has been agreed with the customer, the promised service is provided. This means that the service components booked by the customer must be provided. This results in several tasks for internal groups. These can be the provision of storage space, the setup and maintenance of a database, or even Service Desk support. The services to be provided by an internal group are defined in an operational level agreement (OLA). This is an agreement at the operational, internal level. An OLA should not simply be dictated but rather negotiated and agreed between the groups involved. Before creating an SLA, one should be aware of the performance levels of the groups that will provide it. Otherwise, the customer may be promised round-the-clock support from the Service Desk, for example, but the Service Desk cannot provide this at all. If SLAs are drawn up with customers that exceed the capabilities of the groups tasked with providing the services, this can lead to dissatisfaction among all parties involved: Customers may not receive what they were promised in the SLA and IT staff may be overworked and unable to achieve their goals. All this can lead to frustration as well as increased potential for conflict with the person who agreed the SLAs with the customers.

External service providers are often required to provide a service. A typical example of this would be the provision of a WAN line by a telecommunications service provider. The document in which this service is described is called an underpinning agreement (UA). While an OLA is an internal agreement, a UA is usually a legally binding contract.

Instead of underpinning agreement, the term 'underpinning contract (UC)' is often used to emphasize the contractual meaning.

From the service provider's point of view, this contract is a UA, and from the external service provider's point of view, it is an SLA. The reason for this is that, for example, the WAN line mentioned above is only one component of the overall service for the service provider. For them, it is a means to an end. The sales representative of the telecommunications service provider, on the other hand, refers to its service catalog, from which the service provider selects a WAN line. From the telecommunications service provider's point of view, this is the end product, the service, which is governed by an SLA.

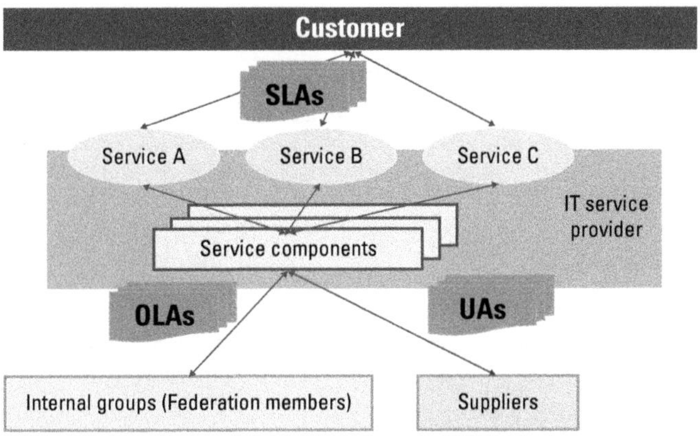

Figure 12: Service agreements and their relationships

To meet the service targets defined in an SLA, the internal and external service providers involved in the service must deliver certain levels of performance. To this end, operational targets are defined and included in the OLA and SLA. The operational target values are therefore derived from the service targets.[9] Regular measurement of the levels delivered enables compliance with the OLA and UA to be checked. These values are also frequently required for regular reports to the customer and can also lead to an adjustment of the service targets in the SLA.

4.3.2 Roles in the process

The **process owner** defines the process objectives for Service Level Management and checks that these are achieved. He bears overall responsibility, appoints the process manager and provides sufficient resources for the process. This process requires more support during initialization and in the start-up phase because the activities are extensive. In addition, the process manager defines the interfaces to other processes. This relates primarily to Customer Relationship Management and Service Portfolio Management.

9 Let's assume that a service consists of five components that are essential for operation. If the customers of this service are promised a service availability of 99.5% (service target), this is just achieved with an availability of the individual components of 99.9% (operational targets).

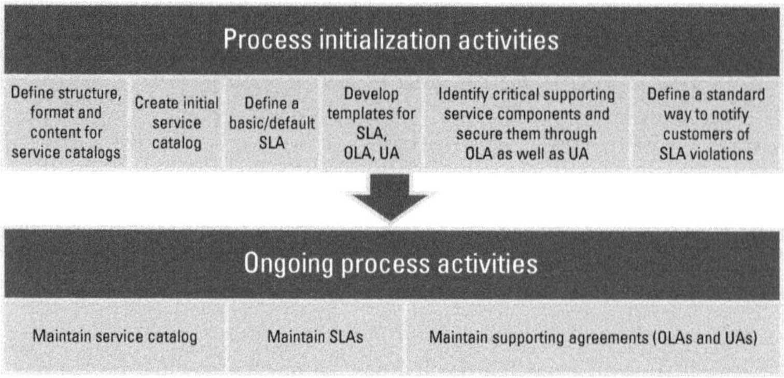

Figure 13: Activities in the Service Level Management process

The operational responsibilities of the **process manager** include:

- Service catalog maintenance, including the management of updates to the service catalog.
- Ensuring that the service catalog is aligned with the service portfolio.
- Negotiation of SLAs with customers.
- Agreement of OLAs with internal groups.
- Negotiation of UAs with external service providers.
- Ensuring that all SLAs, OLAs and UAs are documented in a consistent manner.
- Approving new or modified SLAs.
- Ensuring that SLAs, OLAs and UAs are interlocked.

In addition, there is an **owner for** each **SLA, OLA, and UA** who ensures that the corresponding document is aligned with the specifications, that compliance is checked, that the achievement of objectives is measured, and that the document undergoes a regular review. If the requirements change, it is the owner's task to understand these changes and to incorporate them into the respective document. The generic role model of FitSM describes a role that is frequently encountered in practice ("service manager", "service delivery manager", etc.) as the case owner.

4.3.3 Requirements

For Service Level Management, five requirements are named for the service catalog and for operational service management:

- SLM 2.1: Maintain service catalog;
- SLM 2.2: Agree and regularly review SLAs;
- SLM 2.3: Review service performance;
- SLM 2.4: Agree and regularly review OLAs and UAs;
- SLM 2.5: Review performance of service components.

SLM 2.1: Maintain service catalog

This requirement states the need to establish and maintain a service catalog. By maintaining a service catalog, organizations can provide a clear and standardized overview of their services to both internal stakeholders and external customers. This facilitates transparency, helps in managing customer expectations, and enables effective decision-making regarding service offerings. Additionally, a well-maintained service catalog serves as a valuable reference for service management processes, ensuring that all stakeholders have access to accurate and up-to-date information about the services provided. FitSM recognizes the following capability level descriptions:

Capability level	Description
1	The service provider is able to communicate its service offerings to its customers through some (undefined) format. These services may be described more in terms of technical components than value-generating services as defined by IT service management.
2	There is a list of offerings to customers that attempts to divide these offerings into logical (value-generating) services. This list is maintained on an informal basis.
3	There is a service catalog clearly specifying differentiated service offerings described in terms of value generation for customers. This is maintained based on documented responsibilities.

SLM 2.2: Agree and regularly review SLAs

Contractual arrangements between the customer and IT are made based on the services formulated in the service catalog. In other words, the quality of IT services to be delivered, what customers can expect, and what they must pay for, are all described. These arrangements for the customer are then backed up by the requirements for OLA and UA formulated in PR2.4.

Once the arrangements have been made, they should be reviewed on a regular basis. The service objectives and the concrete achievement of objectives in practice should be considered. There should also be an exchange with the respective customers about how the services are used for their business processes and business objectives. This counteracts the risk of the service provider not noticing that, for example, a 'normal' intranet has become a business-critical IT service with a control function for important processes in the company. Supporting regulations such as OLAs and UAs are described analogously in requirement PR2.4.

Capability level	Description
1	Agreements between the service provider and its customers exist, but do not cover all services for all customers. Service targets are not specified in the agreements. There is no review of SLAs at planned intervals.
2	Agreements for the most important services provided to the most important customers exist and consider service targets. There is however no defined format or structure for SLAs. The specification of service targets may be different in different SLAs and may not support the delivery of value needed by customers. SLAs are reviewed periodically, but the frequency and procedure of reviews is undefined and inconsistent. Responsibilities for SLA reviews are not documented.
3	There are clearly defined and documented responsibilities for negotiating and concluding SLAs. All SLAs follow a defined structure. SLAs are reviewed periodically and systematically. Reviews assess appropriateness, achievability and necessary support from other agreements. Reviews are based on defined and documented responsibilities and records are kept.

SLM 2.3: Review service performance

The actual performance of the services must be evaluated against the service targets defined in the SLA. This evaluation is described in a similar way in Customer Relationship Management (review in the service review together with customers) and Service Reporting (definition of the contents of the reports) processes. The concrete design of the capability levels is as follows:

Capability level	Description
1	Performance is evaluated on a technical level, more aligned to service components and underlying configuration items than services and service targets.
2	Performance is evaluated by service and against service targets. However, service performance evaluation is not systematic, and responsibilities are not clearly set out.
3	Service performance is evaluated in a systematic way, based on documented responsibilities. It is sufficient to support meaningful reporting on the achievement of all service targets defined in SLAs.

SLM 2.4: Agree and regularly review OLAs and UAs

The service targets agreed with the customer (requirement PR2.2) must be backed up by agreements with internal departments (operational level agreements) and external suppliers (underpinning agreements). This applies to supporting services or corresponding service components. FitSM defines service components as "logical part of a service that provides a function enabling or enhancing a service". The service provider can only achieve the service goals and state the needed support for each situation through these agreements.

Just like the agreements with the customer, the assigned agreements with the supporting units (OLA and UA) must be reviewed. This requires a uniform procedure and a coordinated approach.

Capability level	Description
1	OLA- and UA-like agreements exist, but do not cover the majority of service components and supporting services. Operational targets for supporting services or service components are not clearly specified.
2	OLAs and UAs for most service components and supporting services exist and consider service targets. There is however no defined format or structure for OLAs and UAs. Operational target specifications may vary in different OLAs and UAs, and may not be aligned sufficiently to service targets to support the delivery of value needed by customers. There is no consistent review for all necessary OLAs und UAs.
3	The service provider has clearly defined and documented responsibilities for negotiating and concluding OLAs and UAs. All OLAs and UAs follow a defined and uniform structure. They are reviewed at planned intervals. Operational targets are aligned to service targets.

SLM 2.5: Review performance of service components

Just as the performance of services must be evaluated against the agreed targets, the performance of service components must be evaluated against the operational target values defined in the OLAs and UAs. This assessment ultimately ensures that the service targets agreed with the customer are broken down into the individual departments and the IT infrastructure.

Capability level	Description
1	Performance is evaluated on a technical level, more aligned to service components and underlying configuration items than services and service targets.
2	Performance is evaluated by service and against service targets. However, service performance evaluation is not systematic, and responsibilities are not clearly set out.
3	Service performance is evaluated in a systematic way, based on documented responsibilities. It is sufficient to support meaningful reporting on achievement of all service targets defined in UAs and OLAs.

5 Plan and Ensure

Once the IT service provider has formulated its offerings, identified its customers and concluded the contracts, it must ensure delivery. To provide services, the support of suppliers is often required. Availability must be ensured both during normal operations and in exceptional situations like pandemics and other unpredictable emergencies. In IT service management, a series of tasks must be performed for this purpose, which are described in FitSM in three processes:

- Supplier Relationship Management (SUPPM);
- Service Availability & Continuity Management (SACM);
- Capacity Management (CAPM).

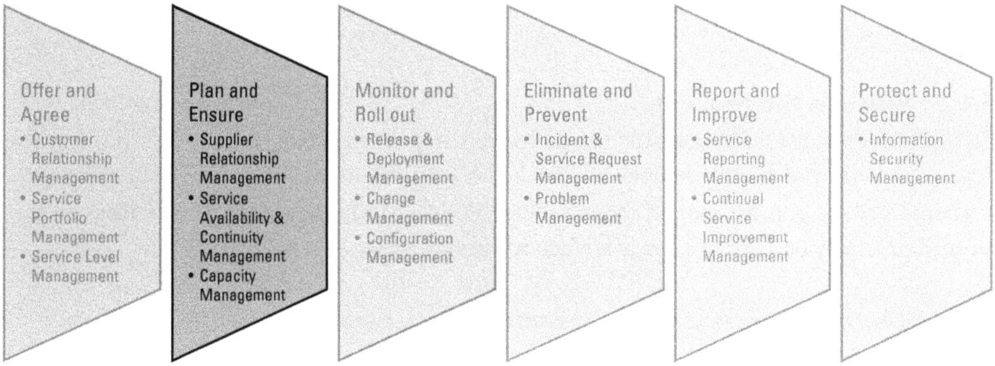

Figure 14: FitSM process model for Plan and Ensure

5.1 SUPPLIER RELATIONSHIP MANAGEMENT

Supplier Relationship Management takes care of establishing and maintaining a healthy relationship with suppliers (internal as well as external) and monitors the contractual performance of services. In practice, this process focuses primarily on external suppliers, although internal suppliers must also be included.

5.1.1 Process description

The service provider must maintain a comprehensive knowledge of all agreements made with suppliers. To facilitate this, an overview is meticulously curated, encompassing all suppliers of products and/or services utilized in service provisioning, along with the corresponding underpinning agreements that have been established.

This database should not only show which agreements exist, what specifically must be provided and when these contracts expire, if applicable. It should also provide information on how to reach the supplier and who within the company maintains contact with the supplier. In addition, this process should check whether a supplier is meeting its contractual obligations. Analogous to Customer Relationship Management, mechanisms for regular communication with suppliers should also be established.

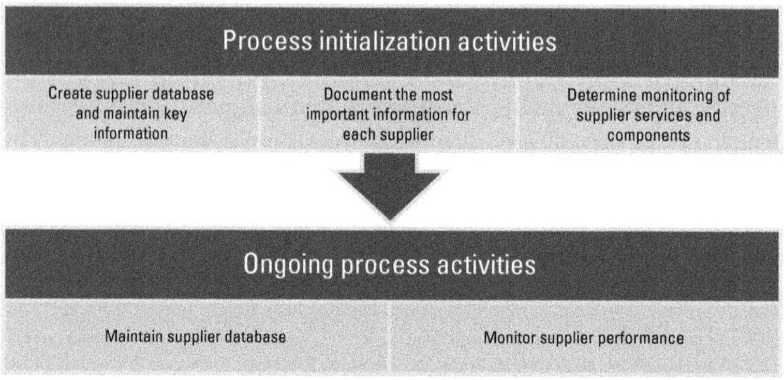

Figure 15: Activities in the Supplier Relationship Management process

5.1.2 Roles in the process

The **process owner** is responsible for defining the process objectives and providing the resources required to achieve these. Since the services of the suppliers (underpinning agreements) are commissioned from Service Portfolio Management, the process owner should precisely coordinate the interface to this process.

The **process manager** appointed by the process owner takes care of:

- Maintaining the supplier database so that the information it contains is up-to-date at all times.
- Ensuring that supplier performance is monitored in accordance with processes.

There is one **supplier relationship manager** for each supplier. The supplier relationship manager is the contact person for a specific supplier, maintains the supplier relationship and develops mechanisms to monitor the supplier's performance. A single supplier relationship manager may well manage several suppliers. In the initialization phase of this process or in the case of smaller IT departments, these roles can be assumed by the process manager themself.

5.1.3 Requirements

The Supplier Relationship Management process is described via four requirements:

- SUPPM 8.1: Identify internal and external suppliers;
- SUPPM 8.2: Establish contact points for suppliers;
- SUPPM 8.3: Establish communication channels with suppliers;
- SUPPM 8.4: Evaluate suppliers regularly.

SUPPM 8.1: Identify internal and external suppliers

As a fundamental step of the process, all suppliers need to be recognized in terms of the objective to be achieved. Analogous to the Customer Relationship Management process, in which the customers must be identified, the suppliers must be recorded. This kind of summary makes clear the commitments that have been established.

Capability level	Description
1	Internal and external suppliers are internally known but there is no formal list of suppliers.
2	There is a list of internal and external suppliers. This list is maintained on an informal basis, without any clear responsibilities for maintaining it or consistent information to be held on each supplier.
3	There is a list of all internal and external suppliers maintained that is based on documented responsibilities.

SUPPM 8.2: Establish contact points for suppliers

Organizational responsibilities must be created to make the relationship with suppliers efficient and effective. These can be specific persons or, if necessary, groups of persons. It is important to have an overarching and uniform definition of how the supplier relationship is to be structured.

Capability level	Description
1	There is no designated contact for each supplier, but individuals from the service provider have a basic understanding of the need to manage relationships with suppliers.
2	There is a person or role generally assigned to each specific supplier or group of suppliers. This assignment is not necessarily based on documented responsibilities, and management of the relationships with the supplier may be inconsistent.
3	There is a person or role assigned to each specific supplier or group of suppliers that manages the relationship based on documented responsibilities.

SUPPM 8.3: Establish communication channels with suppliers

As with communication with customers, channels of communication with suppliers must be structured to ensure effective and efficient ongoing communication between the parties. The type of communication as well as the rhythm must be regulated. If the supplier maintains the relationship on its own initiative in accordance with its Customer Relationship Management, this approach can be adopted. It is only necessary to check whether this is also sufficient from the point of view of IT when acting as the IT service provider. The same applies here: it is important to find and document an internally agreed regulation, ideally in underpinning agreements.

Capability level	Description
1	Communication with suppliers is possible but occurs in a haphazard way and on demand. There is no single clear list of supplier communication channels, and it may prove difficult to communicate with suppliers in a timely manner.
2	There are established communication channels for each supplier, but it is tied to the individual or role assigned to it. The communication channels, including escalation mechanisms, are recorded in some centralized location but not in a consistent way.
3	Communication channels for each supplier, including escalation mechanisms are recorded in a single, consistent way based on documented responsibilities.

SUPPM 8.4: Evaluate suppliers regularly

Monitoring of supplier performance must be ensured. The supplier's contractual obligations and reports should be reviewed in a coordinated manner to ensure that the company's own service targets from the SLA are achieved. For example, there is the possibility of conducting supplier audits or regular reports with coordinated key figures. The service provider should focus on its own perspective and not rely on the supplier's reports without checking them. From the IT review perspective, it is essential to hold meetings with the suppliers and to discuss and question the reports.

Capability level	Description
1	Supplier performance is monitored through informal means. Evaluation is not aligned to agreements with the supplier and more likely focused on technical service components. No reports from the supplier are agreed.
2	Mechanisms that measure supplier performance are used, and to some extent aligned to agreements with the supplier. Evaluation is not systematic and responsibilities are not set out. Some reports may be received from the supplier but they are not consistent or well specified.
3	Mechanisms that measure supplier performance at planned intervals are used, based on documented responsibilities. Evaluation is well aligned to agreements with suppliers, and any reports provided by the supplier are well specified.

■ 5.2 SERVICE AVAILABILITY & CONTINUITY MANAGEMENT

The Service Availability & Continuity Management process is responsible for ensuring sufficient service availability and continuity to meet service targets. This means not only normal, day-to-day operation but also to avoid impacts on services due to disasters and to minimize the negative impact on critical business processes in the event of an exceptional situation.

5.2.1 Process description

Strictly speaking, two sub-processes are considered in this process:

- Service Availability Management:
  Service availability management focuses on availability during normal operation. The availability of a service or service component shows the extent to which it provides the desired functionality at a certain time or over a certain period of time.
- Service Continuity Management:[10]
  Service Continuity management aims to prevent catastrophic events and ensure service functionality even during crises, emergencies, or disasters, whether in part or in full, and to restore services promptly as agreed upon. This entails ensuring continuous functionality during events like floods, earthquakes, fires, pandemics, or prolonged power outages. The goal is to minimize the likelihood and impact of such occurrences, safeguarding the continuity of services.

Technology has changed significantly over recent decades. With virtualization and cloud technologies, continuity needs should be established and the service should be built accordingly. Instead of minimizing occurrence and impact as stated above, it should be related to minimizing the business impact of disasters and service interruption by using modern technology. For example, a highly critical service might be available in redundant or multiple cloud data centers. Hence, the business impact becomes an issue of business continuity: for example, where will personnel work to reach the operational service.

Many measures to increase availability also have a positive effect on emergency preparedness and vice versa. For example, a redundant system at two different locations increases availability in daily operations and reduces the probability of failure in the event of a disaster. It therefore makes sense to combine both aspects in one process.

A large part of the availability and continuity requirements have been agreed in the SLAs with the support of this process and can now be transferred into operation. An availability level and perhaps even corresponding measures for disaster situations have already been agreed with the customer. Nevertheless, there may be reasons to consider further aspects. For example, from a strategic point of view, it may be interesting to show the customer that the quality goes beyond the agreed minimum and this becomes the de facto contracted level.

In the context of availability, various terms are frequently used, the definition of which may differ somewhat depending on the source.

---

10 It is important to emphasise that this is about service continuity management. This process should work closely with business continuity management, because in the event of disasters or similar events, it is not just IT and its services that are affected, but the entire company or the customer.

- Availability:
  Availability is usually measured as a percentage. It indicates the extent to which a service or service component delivers the intended functionality within the agreed service times. Expressed mathematically, this results in:

$$\text{Availability in percent} = \frac{\text{Agreed service time - downtime}}{\text{Agreed service time}} * 100$$

- Time Between Service Incidents:
  Duration between the occurrence of two service incidents. It consists of the downtime and the subsequent operating time until the next failure.
- Downtime (Time to Restore Service):
  Time required after the occurrence of a system fault until a service or component is functioning again as planned. It is made up of detection time and resolution time.
  - Detection Time
    Time required to detect that a component is not available or not performing its function properly.
  - Resolution Time
    The resolution time is the sum of the response time, repair time and recovery time.
    - Response Time
      Time required to be able to start the repair.
    - Repair Time
      Time required to repair a defective component.
    - Recovery time
      If rework is required to reintegrate a repaired component into the infrastructure or into a service, this work is included in the recovery time.

In the event of target values being defined for the terms mentioned, it must be established exactly how the measurement is to be done. This applies if these values are agreed with the customer in the SLA.

An essential part of this process is the identification and handling of risks. A risk is a possible event that has a negative impact on service delivery. To deal with risks, the potential threats must first be identified, their probability of occurrence determined, and finally the impact (damage) assessed. Questions are asked, such as:

- How likely is it that a hard drive in a server will fail or that an airplane will crash into our data center?
- What (financial) impact can be expected for the customer if the ERP system, this server, etc. fails completely or the data center is destroyed?

A simple structure can help to assess the risks. Figure 16 shows a three-level classification that can indicate the importance of managing the risk. The extreme risks must always be addressed in risk management, while those assessed as low risks may be accepted with no formal risk management measures instituted. For services in Risk class 1, for example, concrete agreements could be made in the SLAs and emergency scenarios planned and practiced.

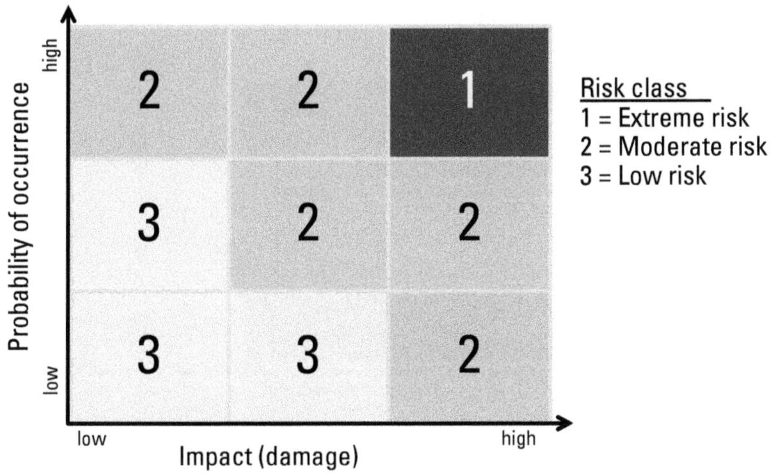

Figure 16: Risk assessment based on risk classes

There are various strategies for dealing with risks. Complete avoidance of a risk is usually not possible in practice. Risks can be reduced by, for example, creating redundancy for error-prone components. Some insurance companies offer the possibility of transferring risks to them through insurance. As a rule, it does not make sense from an economic point of view to avoid, reduce or transfer all risks. It is legitimate to accept certain risks. Nevertheless, decisions must be made and therefore risks must be identified and evaluated, and measures must be defined to minimize the impact on business if the risk materializes.

The handling of a risk and the tasks arising from it are recorded in an availability and continuity plan. This includes the extent to which the measures taken must be subject to regular review.

The actual availability achieved is continuously measured and compared with the targets set. The Service Reporting Management process can be integrated for this purpose.

Plans are important in this process, however FitSM emphasizes content rather than the delivery method. Therefore, FitSM first requires the collection of requirements and focuses on the risks. These requirements and risks must be addressed, including through plans that are an output of the process. For availability, the plans provide good support and guidance in operations. For continuity, the plans are a valuable aid. Plans define what constitutes an emergency and who is allowed to declare it, and which services must be restored first from the customer's point of view. With their targeted activities, they ensure a planned approach in an emergency, despite the increased stress level. If the Cost to mitigate the risk is too high, e.g. no possibility to duplicate some technical parts of the service, the Continuity plan might even be that there is no such plan, and in the case of an emergency, the service will be newly created from scratch. This is also part of the plan and actually exists in a number of situations for a limited part of the service. However, none of the critical services should be addressed in this way.

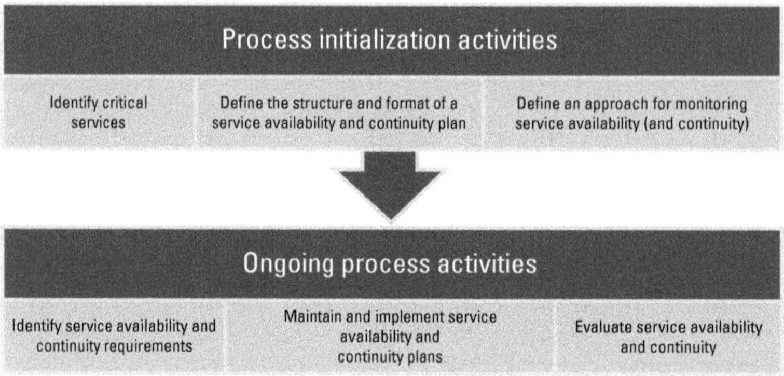

Figure 17: Activities in the Service Availability & Continuity Management process

5.2.2 Roles in the process

When considering the process objectives and the interfaces to other processes, the **process owner** should consider the Customer Relationship Management process and especially the Service Level Management process. Requirements for this process can be derived from Service/Operational Level and Underpinning Agreements. When it comes to reporting, the Service Reporting Management process can provide support.

The **process manager** appointed by the process owner takes care of:

- Identifying availability and continuity requirements.
- Ensuring stakeholders provide the data needed to create availability and continuity plans.
- The creation, maintenance and regular review of all availability and continuity plans.
- Ensuring that measures to improve availability and continuity are implemented, taking into account the Change Management process.
- Serving as the point of contact for availability and continuity issues.

There is one **owner** for each **availability and continuity plan**. His or her tasks include:

- The creation and maintenance of the respective plan.
- Ensuring that all relevant stakeholders are informed in the event of a change.
- Ensuring changes to the plan are approved as needed.
- Ensuring that continuity plans are regularly tested and maintenance work (for example on the emergency power supply) is regularly carried out.

5.2.3 Requirements

There are four requirements for Service Availability & Continuity Management:

- SACM 4.1: Identify and regularly check availability/continuity requirements;
- SACM 4.2: Check availability/continuity risks regularly;
- SACM 4.3: Reduce risks;
- SACM 4.4: Monitor availability.

The first three relate to both availability (normal operation) and continuity (emergency situations). The fourth requirement then relates only to the monitoring of normal operation. Emergency situations occur only sporadically, if at all, so that continuous monitoring is not possible.

SACM 4.1: Identify and regularly check availability/continuity requirements

The requirements for availability and continuity must be derived from the agreements (SLAs) made with the customers. This derivation must be regularly reviewed and adjusted. The possible characteristics of the capability levels are described as follows.

Capability level	Description
1	There is a general understanding of service availability and continuity needs, but there is no consistent and uniform documentation of them.
2	There is a consistent and uniform documentation of service availability and continuity requirements. The approach to requirements identification is mostly infrastructure-focused, only partially addresses service targets or customer needs, or is not performed on a regular basis.
3	There is a consistent and uniform documentation of service availability and continuity requirements. The identification considers SLAs, and the documented requirements are aligned to service targets. They are reviewed at planned intervals.

SACM 4.2: Check availability/continuity risks regularly

This requirement emphasizes the need to assess service availability and continuity risks at planned intervals, especially as technology changes and improves, and business needs change over time. Organizations must conduct systematic evaluations to identify potential risks that could impact the availability and continuity of their services. By conducting these assessments at planned intervals, organizations can stay proactive in their risk management approach and ensure that they are up-to-date with the evolving landscape of potential threats.

Testing continuity plans is crucial to ensure they effectively function when needed. Continuity plans are designed to mitigate risks and ensure business operations can continue in the face of disruptions or disasters. However, without regular testing, there is no guarantee that these plans will work as intended during a real-life incident. Testing continuity plans allows organizations to identify any weaknesses or gaps in their strategies, enabling them to refine and improve their response procedures. This proactive approach not only increases the likelihood of successful recovery but also minimizes potential downtime and associated costs.

Moreover, as IT systems and processes evolve, continuity plans must be updated and adapted accordingly. Regular testing provides an opportunity to validate these updates and ensure they align with the organization's current infrastructure and operational requirements. By testing continuity plans regularly, ITSM teams can maintain confidence in their ability to effectively manage and mitigate disruptions, thereby enhancing overall service availability and reliability. Ultimately, testing continuity plans is essential for organizations to uphold their service commitments and safeguard against potential disruptions that could impact business operations and customer satisfaction.

These assessments enable organizations to identify vulnerabilities, evaluate the effectiveness of existing risk mitigation measures, and identify new risks that may have emerged since the last assessment. FitSM-6 describes the following capability levels.

Capability level	Description
1	Some availability and continuity risks are identified, but the assessment of these risks is irregular and does not follow the same approach for the whole organization. The results of risk assessments are often not easily comparable with each other.
2	Availability and continuity risks are identified. The results of the reasonably regular assessments follow a largely uniform structure (e.g. use the same number of levels for determining probability and impact). However, more detailed procedures are not documented. If assessments are carried out by different persons, the results are not always directly comparable.
3	Availability and continuity risks are identified in a planned manner and with standardized tools (e.g. hazard/threat catalogs). Risks are assessed using clearly defined criteria and procedures that allow for comparability of results.

SACM 4.3: Reduce risks

The requirement stated in PR4.3 highlights the need to take appropriate measures to mitigate the availability and continuity risks while meeting the identified requirements. Organizations must identify potential risks that could affect the availability and continuity of their services and implement measures to minimize both the likelihood and impact of these risks. Organizations must consider the specific requirements related to availability and continuity, such as service level agreements (SLAs) and business continuity plans, and ensure that the implemented measures align with these sources. By proactively addressing availability and continuity risks and meeting the identified requirements, organizations can minimize disruptions, maintain service quality, and provide a reliable and resilient service environment for their stakeholders. These are the capability levels from FitSM-6.

Capability level	Description
1	Some measures to increase availability and continuity are implemented. However, there is no overarching planning and the measures are often not coordinated with each other.
2	Measures to increase availability and continuity are implemented. The planning and implementation of the measures is not always, but often based on previously assessed risks or identified requirements. The impact of the measures on the risks is not always checked and documented.
3	Measures to increase availability and continuity are planned and implemented in a systematic way. This is based on previously assessed risks and identified requirements. The impact of the implementation of the measures on the risks and the fulfilment of the requirements is a central aspect of the planning, implementation and final evaluation of the measures.

SACM 4.4: Monitor availability

The need to monitor the availability of services and their individual components is emphasized in this requirement. Organizations must establish monitoring mechanisms to track and assess the availability of their services in real-time. By monitoring service availability, organizations can promptly identify and address any disruptions or issues that may arise, ensuring that services are consistently accessible to users. By actively monitoring service availability, organizations can proactively respond to incidents, optimize service delivery, and maintain high levels of customer satisfaction.

Capability level	Description
1	Availability monitoring is focused on important technical components. There is little or no aggregation of technical monitoring data into service-based metrics. The approach towards monitoring is more driven by technical capabilities and constraints than by requirements based on customer needs and service targets.
2	For most services delivered to customers, technical monitoring data is aggregated and integrated with other information to enable reporting of end-to-end service availability to some extent.
3	Monitoring follows a clear, consistent and well-documented approach to enable the reporting of end-to-end availability of all services. Information is aggregated and presented in a way to allow straightforward evaluation of service target achievement. The overall approach towards monitoring, the technologies employed as well as aggregation algorithms, heuristics or other methods applied to calculate end-to-end availability are well documented.

5.3 CAPACITY MANAGEMENT

The Capacity Management process is responsible for ensuring that sufficient capacity is provided to meet agreed service capacity and performance requirements.

5.3.1 Process description

The information needed for this process comes from the service level agreements (SLAs) since that's where the services agreed upon with the customers are outlined. If clear capacities are stated, such as the hard disk space provided, the required capacity can be easily derived from this. It becomes more difficult if capacities are expressed indirectly, as is the case, for example, with the maximum number of simultaneous accesses to a website. It becomes even more difficult if no agreements have been made. In practice the question often arises as to which response times of an application still satisfy the users. As in SACM, FitSM focuses on the content of the plans in this process.

When people talk about 'capacity' this often first implies a purely technical perspective. One thinks of free storage space or network bandwidth. But financial and personnel aspects must play a role. For example, the accessibility of the Service Desk depends to an enormous degree on its personnel capacity, and new technical capacities naturally require financial support and lead times for procurement.

Capacity expansion may seem straightforward, particularly in cases such as technical capacity. However, capacity management places significant emphasis on the financial dimension, ensuring that capacity is not only available but also economically efficient. It entails striking a balance between having enough capacity to meet demand without overspending. Therefore, the focus is on ensuring that the required capacity is procured at a reasonable cost, avoiding both excess and insufficiency.

The most important components relevant to capacity are constantly monitored. This can be done at various levels. At the service level, response times of an application can be measured at the end point (client at the user). At the operational level, the focus can be on the performance of the individual servers (free hard disk space, processor performance, memory utilization, network bandwidth used). By defining threshold values and monitoring them automatically, any instance of critical value being exceeded can trigger a warning. In this way, a capacity bottleneck can be reacted to in a timely manner.

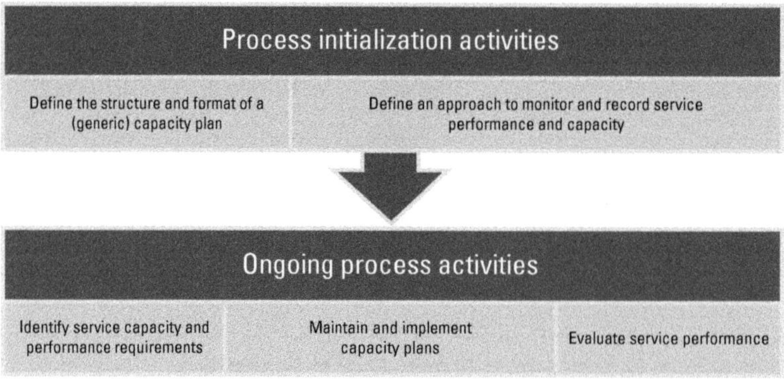

Figure 18: Activities in the Capacity Management process

Capacity plans outline future expansion needs. These plans have two important influencing factors:
- Regularly measured resource utilization indicates future bottlenecks.
- New or modified SLAs show which services are to be provided in the future. This allows conclusions to be drawn about the capacity required.

An important prerequisite for the second point is that customer contact is maintained in the Customer Relationship Management and Service Portfolio Management processes, and any strategic changes or decisions by the customer that are likely to affect capacity are reflected in SLAs. This could be the opening of a new location with new workstations or large special promotions in a web store. FitSM focuses on the content of the plans in this process, as in SACM. The demand must be determined and reviewed as well as the current capacity and utilization.

5.3.2 Roles in the process

The **process owner** should specify the interface to Service Portfolio Management and Service Availability & Continuity Management in more detail since the capacity requirements from the SLAs are an important basis for the work in this process. He defines the process objectives and appoints a **process manager** to plan and implement operational activities. His or her tasks include, in particular:
- Identification of service performance and capacity requirements.
- Ensure stakeholders provide the data needed to create capacity plans.
- Ensure capacity plans are created, maintained and reviewed on a regular basis.
- Ensure that measures to increase service performance and capacity are implemented, taking into account the Change Management process.
- Serve as contact for questions regarding service performance and capacity.

For each **capacity plan** there is a **responsible person (owner)**. His or her tasks include:
- Creation and maintenance of the respective plan.
- Ensure that all relevant stakeholders are informed in the event of a change.
- Ensure changes to the plan are approved as needed.
- Depending on the content of the capacity plan, initiate the creation of change requests (for example, for capacity expansion), or for quality assurance, initiate the Continual Service Improvement process.

5.3.3 Requirements

Four requirements are formulated for capacity management. The structure and formulation of these requirements are deliberately analogous to those in Service Availability & Continuity Management.
- CAPM 5.1: Identify and regularly review capacity/performance requirements;
- CAPM 5.2: Identify current capacity and utilization;
- CAPM 5.3: Plan resources;
- CAPM 5.4: Monitor and analyze performance.

CAPM 5.1: Identify and regularly review capacity/performance requirements
The service goals that are agreed with the customers in the SLAs should always be the main basis for determining the capacity and performance requirements. This has two benefits: The customer can influence the required capacity through prices. For the IT service provider, this gives a clear definition of what must be delivered. These service goals need to be added by a projection. However, it will usually be the case that the customer has to provide these projections. The capability levels for this requirement are as follows:

Capability level	Description
1	There is a general understanding of capacity and performance needs, but there is no consistent and uniform documentation of them.
2	There is consistent and uniform documentation of service capacity and performance requirements. They are not consistently reviewed at planned intervals. The approach to requirements identification is mostly infrastructure-focused and only partially addresses service targets or customer needs.
3	There is consistent and uniform documentation of service capacity and performance requirements. They are reviewed at planned intervals. The determination takes into account SLAs as well as predicted demand.

CAPM 5.2: Identify current capacity and utilization
Ensuring the effective and efficient implementation of requirements necessitates a thorough understanding of current capacity and utilization levels. By systematically assessing these metrics, organizations can proactively identify potential bottlenecks or areas of inefficiency, enabling them to allocate resources more effectively and optimize service delivery. Moreover, by focusing on requirements and identifying pertinent values, organizations can enhance the maturity of their processes. This involves not only clarifying the specific needs and objectives of stakeholders but also aligning them with the capabilities and constraints of existing resources. Through this iterative process of requirement analysis and value identification, organizations can refine their approach to capacity management, ensuring that it remains responsive to evolving business needs while maximizing resource utilization.

Additionally, a structured approach to capacity management facilitates better decision-making and resource allocation. By systematically documenting and analyzing capacity-related data, organizations can make informed decisions about resource investments and prioritize activities based on their potential impact on service delivery. This proactive stance enables organizations to anticipate and address capacity constraints before they become critical, thereby minimizing the risk of service disruptions and enhancing overall operational resilience. Ultimately, by integrating robust capacity management practices into their operations, organizations can optimize resource utilization, improve service reliability, and better support the achievement of business objectives. The following capability levels are provided by FitSM-6 for this purpose:

Capability level	Description
1	Capacity and utilization is identified, but only irregularly, e.g. in the context of planning major infrastructure changes, or when incidents and other events indicate poor performance.
2	For important services and service components, capacity and utilization is determined regularly or even continuously. However, there is no overarching planning for this, nor are the results from the various assessments and measurements combined into an overall picture.
3	The current capacity and utilization is identified. There is basic overarching planning for this, based on an understanding of service requirements and the service infrastructure. Where appropriate, utilization thresholds, warnings and exceptions have been defined for the most important resources. Capacity and utilization levels, service-based and overall, are reported on a regular basis.

CAPM 5.3: Plan resources

This requirement emphasizes the need to plan for future capacity to meet identified requirements, considering human, technical, and financial resources. Organizations must proactively assess their capacity needs to ensure they can effectively meet the demands of their services in the future. This involves considering various factors, including the availability of skilled personnel, technological capabilities, and financial resources required to scale and accommodate future growth. By planning for future capacity, organizations can anticipate potential bottlenecks or resource constraints, and make informed decisions regarding resource allocation, infrastructure investments, and workforce planning and development. This proactive approach enables organizations to maintain operational efficiency, adapt to changing demands, and ensure the continued delivery of high-quality services that meet the identified requirements.

Capability level	Description
1	Capacity plans are technology-focused and mostly limited to technical resources.
2	Capacity planning considers some non-technical resources, but not in a complete and consistent way.
3	Future capacities are planned in consideration of identified requirements. This involves human, technical and financial resources.

CAPM 5.4: Monitor and analyze performance

This requirement directly addresses the monitoring of services and service components. Attention must be paid both to utilization and to operational warnings and exceptions. From a customer's point of view, sufficient capacity of one service component alone is not satisfactory if others are too weakly dimensioned. Therefore, attention must be paid to the entire service in this process as well. It is important to include reports from the service components at an early stage so that an increase can be initiated in a timely manner. Finally, from a business point of view, overcapacities must be monitored so that resources are not kept unused for longer periods.

Capability level	Description
1	Capacity and performance monitoring is focused on important technical components. There is little or no aggregation of technical monitoring data into service-based metrics. The approach towards monitoring is more driven by technical capabilities and constraints than requirements based on customer needs and service targets.
2	For most services delivered to customers, technical monitoring data is aggregated and integrated with other information to enable reporting of service performance and service capacity utilization to some extent. Based on operational monitoring, warnings and exceptions are identified and necessary actions initiated.
3	Performance analysis follows a clear, consistent and well-documented approach to enable reporting on overall performance and capacity utilization for all services. Data collection technologies used, aggregation algorithms, heuristics or other methods are well documented. Operational alerts and exceptions are identified and recorded in a clearly defined manner.

6 Monitor and Roll out

An orderly transition of new or changed services into operation is ensured by following the three processes listed below. They ensure secure management of the IT infrastructure for the provision of services by allowing changes to proceed in a planned manner, regulating tests and acceptances, and supporting decisions on changes in a targeted manner by means of a consistent model of the IT infrastructure. The aim of these processes is to protect the production environment, while at the same time ensuring necessary and sensible changes and the required flexibility.

The following processes are designed to achieve these objectives and activities:

- Release & Deployment Management (RDM);
- Change Management (CHM);
- Configuration Management (CONFM).

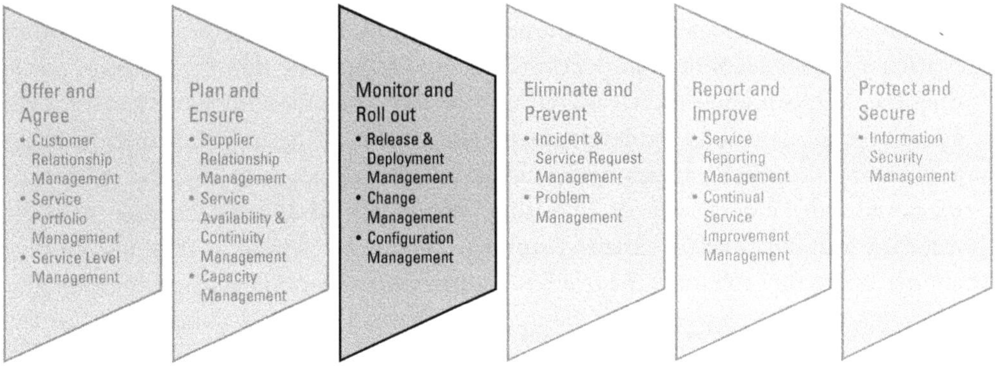

Figure 19: FitSM process model for Monitor and Roll out

6.1 RELEASE & DEPLOYMENT MANAGEMENT

Sometimes it does not make sense to develop changes individually and roll them out directly after completion, but instead to bundle similar changes. They are combined into a logical unit called a 'release'. All changes in a release are tested and transferred to the live environment together. Due to the increased complexity, releases are handled in a separate process, known as Release & Deployment Management. This complements the Change Management process, which handles the individual changes.

6.1.1 Process description

Bundling several changes into a single release is a good idea if the individual changes are closely related or can only be rolled out together in a meaningful way.

The framework and the process of a release, from planning to implementation to completion, is formed by a release guideline. Among other things, it defines exactly what the release entails and which steps are to be performed in sequence to complete it. This often involves the following process:

- Release planning:
  Resource requirements are planned, which includes scheduling, calculating the financial resources required, and identifying the people needed for implementation.
- Release compilation:
  All changes belonging to the release are identified. Sometimes it can be useful to submit further changes and to integrate them in instances where approval is required. This is especially the case when platforms are newly rolled out and the components running on them can be updated relatively easily at the same time.
- Acceptance test:[11]
  In modern testing methodologies, the acceptance test plays a crucial role, concentrating on the technical process to ensure software quality and user satisfaction. Establishing clear acceptance criteria upfront is paramount during the software development phase. These criteria serve as benchmarks against which the software's performance and functionality are evaluated during the acceptance test. Engaging customers and other pertinent stakeholders in this process is essential to validate that the software meets their requirements and expectations effectively. Moreover, the acceptance test serves as a pivotal stage in the software development lifecycle, providing an opportunity to detect and rectify any discrepancies or deficiencies before deployment. By involving end-users and stakeholders early in the testing process, organizations can gather valuable feedback, enabling them to refine and improve the software iteratively. This collaborative approach not only enhances the overall quality of the software but also fosters a sense of ownership and engagement among stakeholders, ultimately contributing to the successful adoption and utilization of the software solution.
- Acceptance evaluation:
  The results of the acceptance test(s) are evaluated to determine the extent to which the release meets the acceptance criteria. In addition, other requirements may be reviewed. For example, an operations manual may be required that describes for administrators how users and rights are managed.

---

11 Some more tests may be necessary, such as performance test, capacity test, resilience test, penetration test, backup and recovery, emergency scenario test, usability test and many more. Identification and proper execution of the necessary tests, form an important basis for stable services.

- Rollout planning:
  In practice, the rollout is often carried out in phases. Unfortunately, this cannot always be achieved, which leads to a rollout in the form of a big bang (i.e., everything at the same time). The associated risk increases immensely, because in the event of a failure not only the workability of a manageable area, but also that of a complete organization can be endangered. Target computers could pull software on demand or a forced installation is set. If there are only a few computers, then a manual installation is an option; if there are many, an automatic rollout will make more sense.
- Rollout preparation:
  The hardware and software to be implemented must be transmitted to the target site. Preparations must be made to minimize the impact on services and customers in the event of an unsuccessful implementation.
- Rollout:
  During the rollout, teams on site may need to be coordinated and the correct process monitored. The rollout ends with a review of whether the release has been successfully implemented. This largely coincides with the review of the successful implementation of the individual changes in Change Management (Post Implementation Review).

Even though the process sounds very formal and much like a traditional waterfall model, it can be applied to agile development methods. Integrating DevOps principles into IT service management, particularly within the Release & Deployment Management process, involves leveraging automation and testing to streamline service delivery and improve overall efficiency. By adopting DevOps practices, organizations can break down silos between development and operations teams, thus fostering collaboration and communication throughout the service lifecycle. Automation plays a pivotal role in this integration, enabling the rapid and consistent deployment of software releases while reducing the risk of human error. Through automated testing processes, such as continuous integration and continuous delivery (CI/CD), organizations can ensure that changes to services are thoroughly tested before deployment, thereby enhancing reliability and minimizing service disruptions. Moreover, by embracing a culture of continuous improvement and feedback, organizations can iteratively enhance their release and deployment processes, aligning with DevOps principles of agility and responsiveness to customer needs. Overall, integrating DevOps into IT service management empowers organizations to deliver high-quality services more efficiently, with automation and testing playing key roles in achieving this objective. The Release & Deployment Management process is one of the key entry points for this.

6.1.2 Roles in the process

In the same way that every process in FitSM has a process owner, the **RDM process owner** is accountable for all generic tasks in context of Release & Deployment Management. This includes acting as the primary contact point for concerns in the context of governing one specific ITSM process and defining and approving goals and

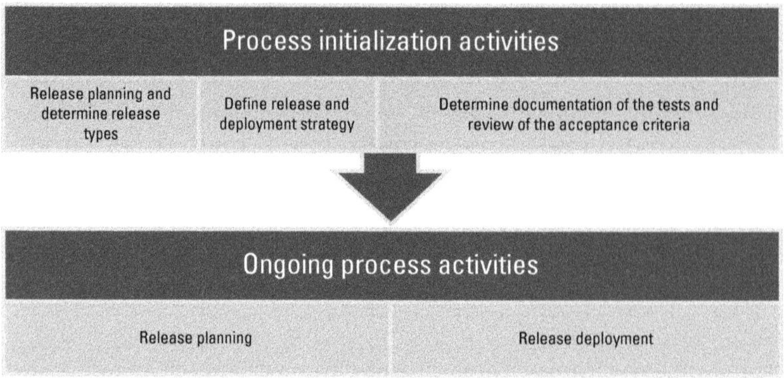

Figure 20: Activities in the Release & Deployment Management process

policies in the context of the process according to the overall SMS goals and policies. When considering the interfaces to other processes, they must look above all at the Change Management process. In addition, they plan the resources for their process, define the goals, and appoint a **process manager** to be responsible for the operational implementation of the process. To this end, they define process activities, assign these to persons or roles, and plan tool support.

The **process manager** owns all of the generic tasks of a process manager in addition to maintaining the overall release planning (including release cycles) and reviewing deployed releases to gauge their success.

Each release is assigned a **release owner**. Their tasks include:

- Controlling and coordinating activities in the lifecycle of the specific release, including planning, building, testing and rollout.
- Ensuring that the required documentation is complete and of adequate quality.
- Acting as a single point of contact on the release for all stakeholders, including the change manager, affected change owner, software developer, issue manager, and customer representatives.

6.1.3 Requirements

For Release & Deployment Management, the following requirements are placed on this process:

- RDM 13.1: Define release and deployment strategy;
- RDM 13.2: Define criteria for including changes in a release;
- RDM 13.3: Plan acceptance criteria and deployment;
- RDM 13.4: Create, test and accept releases;
- RDM 13.5: Plan failure scenario;
- RDM 13.6: Evaluate success.

RDM 13.1: Define release and deployment strategy

This process involves many activities that must be sensibly planned, agreed upon and coordinated. For this purpose, it makes sense to specify a uniform guideline that is valid for all participants. This release policy usually contains general specifications regarding the type, frequency and scheduling of releases. It can specify that, in connection with business-critical services, no releases may be carried out during business hours, except in justified and exceptional cases. Therefore, release policies can exist per application or service, not just the policy for the release process.

Capability level	Description
1	There is some awareness about the various possible approaches towards release and deployment, but no strategy.
2	Approaches to release and deployment have been explored for some parts of the service infrastructure. The feasibility and, where applicable, the advantages and disadvantages of different methods and techniques have been discussed, e.g., fixed provisioning time windows vs. continuous provisioning. Formal or informal strategies are established for individual areas.
3	There are comprehensive release and provisioning strategies based on examining the feasibility, advantages, and disadvantages of different approaches for different parts of the service infrastructure. The strategies are aligned with each other and provide the framework for the assessment and frequency of releases, as well as for the use of deployment technologies.

RDM 13.2: Define criteria for including changes in a release

As part of a release and deployment strategy, the procedure for merging individual changes into a release should be defined. In some organizations, only software changes are integrated. However, it may be important to replace hardware before new software is rolled out. Will the hardware changes be part of the release? Or will the hardware changes be implemented outside of the release?

Capability level	Description
1	How approved changes are included in a release is decided on a case-by-case basis.
2	Incorporating approved changes into a release is usually done in a consistent and planned manner. However, approaches from different parts of the organization may not be aligned and clear criteria are not defined
3	The criteria for including approved changes in a release are clearly defined taking into consideration the applicable release and deployment strategies.

RDM 13.3: Plan acceptance criteria and deployment

Before a release can be tested and accepted, acceptance criteria must be created. Guidance should set out how acceptance criteria are created and who is involved. The procedure for rollout planning should be defined.

Capability level	Description
1	Planning for the deployment of new releases is done on a case-by-case basis.
2	The deployment of new releases is planned, usually, but perhaps not always, taking into account defined acceptance criteria. However, clear guidelines on how to plan the deployment of new releases are not documented.
3	There is clear documented guidance on what to consider when planning the deployment of new releases, including guidance on defining and verifying acceptance criteria.

RDM 13.4: Create, test and accept releases

Acceptance must be granted for each release of a service. This is based on the plan defined in RDM 13.3. It is done after appropriate tests based on acceptance criteria. All relevant parties must be involved in the creation of the acceptance criteria, the tests and the final release.

Capability level	Description
1	Building and testing releases as well as evaluating acceptance is done on a case-by-case basis.
2	A consistent approach has been established for building, testing and evaluating releases, but it is not sufficiently documented and may not always adequately address the impact on services.
3	There are clear guidelines for building, testing, and evaluating releases. These include requirements for release testing, which are graded according to the type of release and the potential impact on services.

RDM 13.5: Plan failure scenario (back out plan)

Protecting live operation in service of the business is of paramount importance in Release and Deployment. Therefore, it is necessary to plan how the business will continue to function in the event of problems with the deployment. This aim is to reduce the impact on services and customers.

Capability level	Description
1	Whether or not reversals of release deployments are planned in advance depends solely on ad-hoc decisions by the people involved.
2	In general, activities are planned and tested for reversing unsuccessful release deployments. However, the approach towards this is not documented and therefore might vary from release to release.
3	For all releases, or for each release type, there is a documented approach towards the planning and testing of activities necessary for reversing an unsuccessful deployment.

RDM 13.6: Post Implementation Review

After the operational execution of the release, it must be checked whether the activities were successful. For this purpose, the acceptance criteria must be taken into account.

Capability level	Description
1	Deployment activities are not consistently monitored for success or failure.
2	In general, the success (or lack thereof) of the deployment is documented. However, the format of documentation might vary. An analysis of the results might or might not be performed.
3	The success or failure of deployment activities is documented in consistent records. The collected information is used for analysis purposes, e.g., to evaluate and further improve the effectiveness of Release and Deployment Management.

6.2 CHANGE MANAGEMENT

There are many reasons for making changes to the components relevant to service provision. From the introduction of a new service or capacity expansions, to the replacement of defective components, these changes are daily business for an IT service provider. At this point it should be noted that a change is a modification (such as addition, removal, modification or replacement) to a configuration item. Change Management ensures that such changes are planned, approved, implemented and reviewed in a controlled manner to avoid any adverse impact on services or customers.

6.2.1 Process description

The Change Management process is responsible for controlling all changes to relevant service components. It is responsible for ensuring that changes are only implemented if they make sense for the organization and also considers the economic dimension. The scope and consequences of a change are identified and the documentation is updated.

A standardized approach to implementing changes brings several advantages. It increases the possibility of a correct and functional implementation and minimizes the risks to productive IT services. This leads to an increase in productivity for users through more stable services.

In determining which aspects of service provision are deemed significant enough to be governed by the Change Management process, organizations must tailor their approach to suit their specific needs and priorities. One approach involves considering customer requirements, which can be derived from Service Level Agreements (SLAs) if necessary. Additionally, organizations should assess their internal IT infrastructure to identify components that warrant inclusion in the Change Management process. These components, known as configuration items (CIs), are defined and managed through the Configuration Management process, where their attributes and relationships are meticulously documented and monitored for changes.

Furthermore, the Configuration Management process plays a pivotal role in maintaining the accuracy and integrity of the configuration items throughout their lifecycle. It involves activities such as configuration identification, control, status accounting, and verification, ensuring that organizations have a comprehensive understanding of their IT infrastructure and its dependencies. By aligning the Change Management process with the Configuration Management process, organizations can effectively assess the impact of proposed changes on configuration items, minimize risks, and maintain service continuity. This integrated approach facilitates efficient change control and enhances overall service delivery and reliability.

A Change usually starts with a Request for Change (RFC). This is a documented proposal for a change to one or more configuration items. A Request for Change must be recorded. It should be able to answer a range of questions, including:

- Which element(s) are to be changed?[12]
- What should be changed about it?
- Is there a date by which the change must be implemented?
- What other components are affected by this change?
- For what reason should the change be made, i.e. what is the business benefit/ value of the change?
- What happens if the change is not implemented?
- What are the costs of the change?
- Who is responsible for the change?
- Who makes the change?
- Who must be informed after the change has been made?

The selection and level of detail of the information to be captured depends on the complexity of the infrastructure and the desired level of control of the organization. It is perfectly possible to keep the scope of documentation smaller for a simple minor change rather than for a major change, which can have a significant impact on the customer.

Using the information provided about the proposed change, it can be classified into one of a set of predefined categories. Classification can provide opportunities for statistical evaluation of the change and assist in selecting the appropriate path that the change should follow from thereon. For example, different people may be involved in a hardware change compared to a software change. As part of the classification, a change should also be assigned a priority, which supports scheduling.

The requested change must then be evaluated for approval or rejection. Can the potential risks be assessed? Are the costs and benefits in reasonable proportions? In order to answer such questions, it can be useful to form a team that jointly discusses whether the change should be approved or rejected. This team is called the Change Advisory Board, or CAB for short. The persons involved should cover all competencies relevant for the

12 Linking the change request to the elements to be changed can significantly support error analysis through the Incident & Service Request Management and Problem Management processes.

evaluation of the change. This also includes the competence to decide who will bear the costs. Whether the change is approved or rejected is documented in the change record.

The modern concept of the Change Advisory Board (CAB) is often misunderstood, with some viewing it solely as a bureaucratic hurdle rather than a strategic decision-making body. It's crucial to recognize that the CAB serves as a forum for evaluating proposed changes comprehensively, ranging from small maintenance updates to significant infrastructure improvements. Rather than solely focusing on deployment approvals, the CAB's primary function lies in assessing the feasibility, risks, and potential impacts of proposed changes before they proceed to implementation. In this context, the CAB acts as a gatekeeper, ensuring that changes align with organizational objectives and minimize disruptions to business operations.

In today's dynamic business environment, organizations must strike a balance between agility and risk management when it comes to Change Management processes. While smaller maintenance changes may be approved within individual departments to expedite operational efficiency, larger-scale changes affecting applications, services, or infrastructure demand a more thorough evaluation by the CAB. This distinction underscores the importance of tailoring the CAB's role to the complexity and potential impact of proposed changes. By involving business executives in CAB discussions, organizations can ensure that proposed changes align with strategic business goals and are evaluated from a holistic perspective, considering not only technical feasibility but also business implications and stakeholder interests.

Moreover, a modern CAB should function as a collaborative platform that fosters communication and consensus-building among stakeholders. Rather than operating as a siloed entity focused solely on technical considerations, the CAB should facilitate cross-functional dialog, drawing upon the expertise of various departments and disciplines. By incorporating diverse perspectives and expertise into the change evaluation process, organizations can make more informed decisions and mitigate the risks associated with change implementation. Ultimately, the modern CAB serves as a critical governance mechanism that balances the need for innovation and agility with the imperative of maintaining operational stability and security.

Once a request for change (RFC) has been approved, the implementation of the change commences. Simple changes, such as a straightforward hardware replacement, are carried out under the leadership of Change Management. If the change is extensive, implementation is carried out through the Release & Deployment Management process, via which the required components are created and tested. This applies not only to software changes, but also to extensive hardware changes. In the Release & Deployment Management process, steps are then also planned to reverse unsuccessful, extensive changes. Such planning is not mandatory for simple changes within the scope of Change Management.

Each implemented change ends with a Post Implementation Review (PIR), a review of the extent to which the desired result has been achieved. Depending on the change, a Post Implementation Review can be very short and simple, or complex and extended.

Typically, three main categories of Changes are distinguished:
- Standard Change;
- Non-Standard Change (Normal Change);
- Emergency Change.

The Standard Change serves to reduce the administrative effort in the day-to-day area. It is a low-risk change that occurs relatively frequently, such as providing basic equipment to a new employee. It follows a predetermined procedure or work instruction and has successfully gone through the change process once. Standard Changes are preauthorized, so no change requests are required to implement them. They are initiated through other mechanisms, such as a call to the Service Desk (a service request).

All Non-Standard Changes go through the activities described previously, starting with the change request (RFC).

Some changes may need to be implemented extremely quickly and there may not be enough time to complete a Non-Standard Change. For example, this may occur if services that support the customer's core processes are down due to defective configuration items, or if a security patch has to be applied as quickly as possible. In such a case, an Emergency Change is initiated. Since these are not Standard Changes, the change can be associated with high risks. In anticipation of the need for Emergency Changes, separate procedures should be defined in advance that take into account both the urgency and the quality required.

A change schedule, also called a schedule of change, records dates and other details for planned changes. The change schedule should be viewable by all stakeholders. The scheduling of changes is simplified by defining time windows (maintenance windows), if possible, across all services. It is also possible to specify a period during which no changes may be made.

6.2.2 Roles in the process

In addition to defining the process objectives and providing the corresponding resources and appointing a process manager, the **process owner** should in particular regulate the interfaces to the two adjacent processes:
- Configuration Management:
  The determination of which changes are to be formally treated as a change and must therefore formally pass through the Change Management process is decided in the Configuration Management process on the basis of the Change Management specifications.

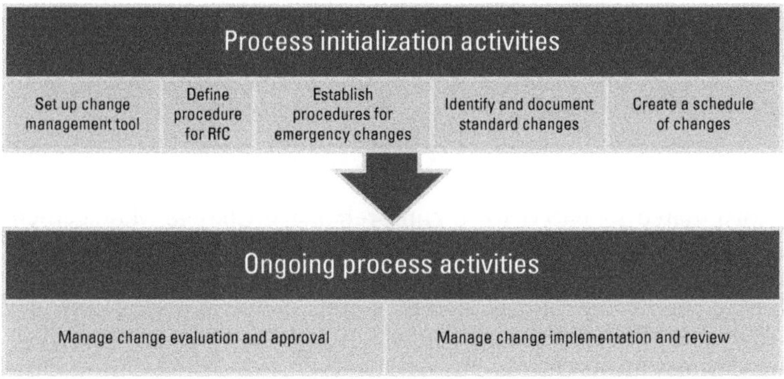

Figure 21: Activities in the Change Management process

- Release & Deployment Management:
  If it is determined that a change can be assigned to a release, implementation is carried out as part of Release & Deployment Management. When reconciling these two processes, it is particularly important to determine what is considered a release.

The operational duties of the **process manager** include the following:
- Plan, schedule, prepare and moderate Change Advisory Board (CAB) meetings.
- Maintenance of the list and descriptions of Standard Changes, in conjunction with the technical specialists.
- Ensure change requests are processed in a timely and effective manner.
- Monitor progress of the review, approval, and implementation of changes.
- Review change records on a regular basis to identify trends, nonconformities, lack of documentation, and poor traceability.

For each change request there is a requester **(change requester)**. They create the change request and add additional information for the change manager. As a rule, they represent the change request in the CAB meeting.

Each change is represented by its own **change owner**. This can be the requestor or another person. They guide the change from approval to completion and takes care of:
- Control and coordination of all activities over the entire lifecycle of the specific change.
- Progress monitoring of the change review and implementation.
- Ensuring that change records are consistently complete and up-to-date, from capture through to Post Implementation Review.
- Communication with the person responsible for the release when the change is implemented as part of a release.

The composition of the **Change Advisory Board (CAB)** depends on the required competencies. Depending on the changes to be evaluated, all persons who can meaningfully contribute to the review and approval should be involved. For each change, the CAB examines the benefits, the risks, the possible effects, the technical feasibility as well as the effort and costs. Based on these factors, the CAB decides on the approval and thus on the implementation of the change.[13]

6.2.3 Requirements

Six requirements are formulated in FitSM for a comprehensive Change Management process:

- CHM 12.1: Record and classify changes uniformly;
- CHM 12.2: Define uniform procedure;
- CHM 12.3: Evaluate changes uniformly;
- CHM 12.4: Approve changes uniformly
- CHM 12.5: Carry out PIR as required and close changes uniformly;
- CHM 12.6: Maintain schedule of changes.

CHM 12.1: Record and classify changes uniformly

The process can only achieve its objectives if all changes are processed through its flow. This is the only way to ensure that no change bypasses the process. The basic prerequisite for this is that all changes are recorded. Classification is used for efficient control of the process. The following capability levels are documented.

Capability level	Description
1	Not all changes are registered; some are handled without the creation of any record. Existing change records vary significantly in format and level of detail.
2	The majority of changes are registered and classified. While there is an intuitive understanding about the information to be collected and method of recording, this is not clearly defined, and responsibilities are not documented.
3	All changes are registered and classified. Recording is based on documented responsibilities and procedures, and the information is recorded in a consistent way. Classification follows a clear scheme and a defined set of criteria, considering different types of changes, including emergency changes and major changes.

CHM 12.2: Define uniform procedure

An agreed and generally applicable scheme must be found for the assessment and approval of change requests. The necessary information must be described, and possible approval hierarchies must be taken into account. If necessary, smaller, low-risk changes can be assessed and approved more easily than extensive ones. In detail, this leads to the following capability levels.

—

13 Depending on the practical implementation, in the event of an Emergency Change, convening the CAB could be too burdensome. In order to speed up the approval process, it would be possible to establish a smaller Emergency Change Advisory Board (ECAB), which quickly assesses Emergency Changes. The ECAB then represents a subset of the CAB that is relevant in an emergency. This approach is neither a requirement nor an explicit recommendation of FitSM. However, it is FitSM compliant.

Capability level	Description
1	Changes are identified and carefully handled in order to avoid malfunctions. The process is mostly random. Responsibilities are not always clear. The steps are defined ad hoc for each change and can vary greatly for comparable changes.
2	There is a procedure for each type of change. Everyone involved knows the steps and usually follows them, even if the process is not consistently documented. The important key points in the implementation of a change are mostly recorded.
3	There is a documented procedure for each type of change. All participants know the steps and follow them. Important key points in the realization of a change are consistently recorded.

CHM 12.3: Evaluate changes uniformly

It is important that changes are evaluated before a decision is made on their implementation. This should not be too time-consuming. The costs and benefits must be weighed up. The risks and possible positive/negative effects must be assessed and technical feasibility is a central part of the assessment process.

Capability level	Description
1	Although changes are usually assessed, this is generally done in a haphazard way. Responsibilities are not always clear. The assessment criteria are defined on an ad hoc basis for each change and can vary greatly between comparable changes. Benefits, risks, potential impacts, effort, and technical feasibility are only partially considered.
2	At least at a general level, there is a largely undocumented consensus on how, by whom and according to which criteria, changes are to be assessed, which is generally adhered to. Benefits, risks, potential impacts, effort and technical feasibility are usually, but not always, taken into account.
3	All changes are reliably assessed according to a defined approach based on documented guidelines and/or procedures. Consideration of benefits, risks, potential impacts, effort and technical feasibility are a core part of the assessment procedure.

CHM 12.4: Approve changes uniformly

An agreed and generally valid scheme must be found for the approval of change requests. It is important to consider who needs to be involved in the decision. Which approvals should be authorized at which hierarchy level? It may be easier to assess and approve smaller changes than larger ones.

Capability level	Description
1	Changes are approved, but in a mostly haphazard way. Responsibilities are not always clear. Approval criteria are set on an ad hoc basis for each change and can vary widely between similar changes.
2	At least at a general level, there is a largely undocumented consensus about how, by whom and according to what criteria, changes should be approved, which is generally adhered to.
3	Approval of all changes follows a defined and documented approach, including clear guidance on the determination of the appropriate level of approval based on the results of the change assessment.

CHM 12.5: Carry out PIR as required and close changes uniformly

Just as in Release & Deployment Management where the release must be checked for success or failure after implementation, a change must also be checked after its implementation. Smaller changes can be considered with a glance at a summarized presentation, larger changes in the context of extensive projects require a more detailed review.

Capability level	Description
1	After the implementation of a change, it is reviewed on an individual basis, following no defined guidelines or criteria. There may be a significant number of changes for which no Post Implementation Review is performed at all.
2	The majority of changes are subject to a Post Implementation Review, following a set of mostly undefined and undocumented, but well understood actions and criteria. To some extent, the results of Post Implementation Reviews are recorded. However, these records do not follow a clear and uniform format.
3	For every change that is implemented, a Post Implementation Review is performed as needed. All Post Implementation Reviews are conducted according to clearly defined guidelines, criteria and/or procedures leading to comparable results, which are documented in a uniform and consistent way.

CHM 12.6: Maintain schedule of changes

Approved changes with the scheduled dates for implementation must be maintained in a schedule of changes or 'change calendar'. This schedule must be made available to all relevant parties. This can be done by providing an overview. A distinction is made between the three capability levels.

Capability level	Description
1	While deployment of changes is usually announced to interested parties, there is no complete and coherent schedule of change maintained.
2	There is a schedule of change accessible to all interested parties, but it might not include all relevant changes or important details.
3	There is a complete and accurate schedule of changes accessible to all interested parties. Schedule entries include relevant details and the proposed deployment date for every approved change.

6.3 CONFIGURATION MANAGEMENT

Many FitSM processes require information about the elements relevant to service delivery and an understanding of how they are interrelated. Configuration Management documents these elements, the so-called configuration items (CI), and their relationships to each other. It ensures that this documentation is always up-to-date.

6.3.1 Process description

The elements to be documented (configuration items (CI)) are objects that contribute to the provision of one or more services or service components and must therefore be subject to a certain level of control. The Configuration Management process documents these CIs in a central database, the Configuration Management Database (CMDB). The CMDB can also be a 'logical' database that bundles configuration information from multiple information sources. The CIs are related to each other, creating a logical map of the services and relevant components, which also represents the dependencies.

A CI can come in diverse forms:

- Hardware:
  A CI can be, for example, a server or just a hardware component such as a hard disk.
- Software:
  For example, an operating system, application, or interface software.
- Cloud Infrastructure:
  This comes primarily in the following forms: Software-as-a-Service (SaaS), Platform-as-a-Service (PaaS), Infrastructure-as-a-Service (IaaS).
- Documentation:
  If a contingency plan is identified as a component relevant to service delivery, it too can be included in the CMDB.
- Services:
  The inclusion of a service makes it possible to link the components (CIs) to the service, on which the service depends.

As diverse as the types of CIs can be, so can their relationships to each other. The following relationships, among others, are common:

- A is a component of B:
  A hard disk system as a component of a server.
- A is connected to B:
  Application server A is connected to database server B.
- A triggers B:
  A virtualization platform automatically starts various virtual machines at startup.
- A is installed on B:
  A software is installed on a particular server.
- A uses B:A server uses a specific storage system to store data.
- A is dependent on B
  A service is dependent on a specific server. If the server fails, the service can no longer be provided.

The configuration of a CI results from the characteristics of the attributes, the relationships and other relevant properties. By the configuration of a printer, for example, FitSM means all the information recorded for this printer in the CMDB. It can also make sense to combine several CIs into one configuration. For example, the configuration of a server is derived from its components and their relevant properties (e.g. server, RAID controller, hard disks).

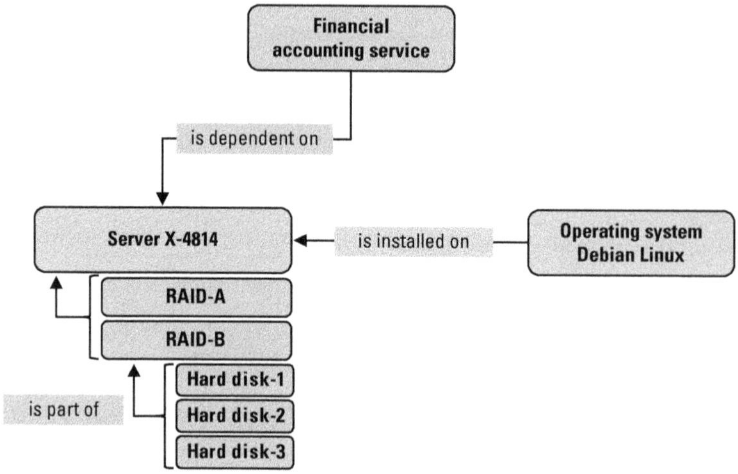

Figure 22: Sample section of a CMDB (from service to configuration item)

For some CIs it may be useful to define a basic configuration (configuration baseline). This minimizes the diversity of configurations and simplifies documentation. For example, if a configuration baseline is defined for workstations, the details no longer have to be recorded for each individual computer. If necessary, a note on potential deviations from the configuration baseline is sufficient.

Critical success factors

Defining a meaningful data model is immensely important. A level of detail that is too low does not capture the essential components and information, which then runs the risk of not receiving the necessary attention. Particularly in the case of changes to components, this can mean that consequences cannot be assessed, and important services are unintentionally influenced.

Too high a level of detail unnecessarily increases the documentation effort. All CIs with all their attributes must be kept up-to-date. Even the inclusion of a single attribute can increase the effort required immensely. If, for example, the build number is recorded for an operating system, it is hardly possible to import an update, no matter how small, without having to update the CMDB.

CMDB: physical and virtual design

There is only one CMDB, and at the same time there can be many of them. What sounds like a contradiction can actually be true and even make sense. The CMDB is the central place for storing all components relevant to service delivery. But what happens if there are already several databases in which this information is distributed? In such a case, consolidation options need to be examined. Anything that can be meaningfully combined reduces complexity. If several databases remain, they are referred to as a physical CMDB. A logical construct, a kind of data warehouse, can be placed on top of them. This has the consequence that logically it looks as if there is only one database. In fact, there are several physical databases underneath. In this case, it is in fact one logical and several physical CMDBs.

The basic task of Configuration Management is therefore not the configuration of hardware and software, but rather to:

- Identify what is to be captured as a CI with which attributes.
- Record the CIs and keep the records up-to-date.
- Identify, document and keep current the relationships between CIs.
- Provide an understanding of the current configuration with the resulting logical representation of the infrastructure.
- Provide all other processes with this information.

In practice, keeping the CMDB up-to-date is a major challenge. For example, a target/actual comparison must be performed regularly (what is documented in the CMDB, what is actually present in the real environment) or an automated inventory must be set up. In addition, the procedure for dealing with the data found must always be regulated.

Cloud environment

In managing configuration within cloud environments, Configuration Management adopts a proactive approach to ensure the seamless operation and optimization of cloud-based services. One example of how Configuration Managers handle configuration management in the cloud is by leveraging Infrastructure as Code (IaC) tools and practices. By defining infrastructure configurations in code, Configuration Managers can automate the provisioning and management of cloud resources, streamlining deployment processes and reducing the risk of configuration drift. Through version control systems and automated deployment pipelines, Configuration Managers can track changes to infrastructure configurations, enforce consistency across environments, and rapidly roll back changes if necessary. Additionally, Configuration Managers may implement configuration management platforms specifically designed for cloud environments, providing centralized visibility and control over configuration settings across multiple cloud providers and services.

Furthermore, Configuration Managers utilize cloud-native configuration management solutions to dynamically adjust resource configurations in response to changing workload demands and performance requirements. For example, auto-scaling features offered by cloud providers allow Configuration Managers to automatically adjust compute resources based on predefined thresholds, ensuring optimal performance and cost-efficiency. Configuration Managers also employ configuration monitoring and auditing tools to continuously assess the compliance and security of cloud environments, identifying and remedying misconfigurations or vulnerabilities promptly. By combining automation, orchestration, and monitoring capabilities, Configuration Managers can effectively manage configurations in the cloud, facilitating agility, scalability, and reliability in service delivery.

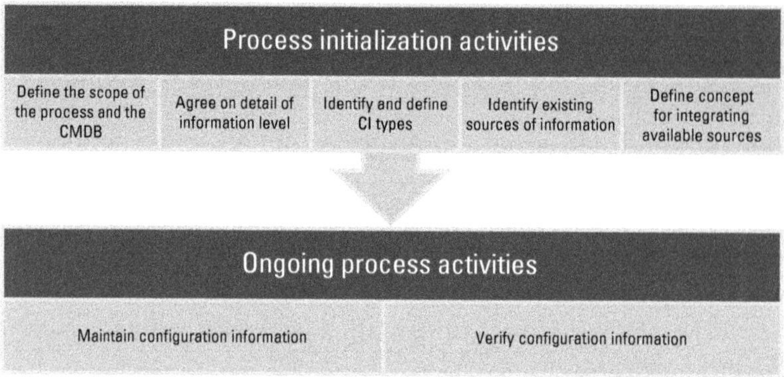

Figure 23: Activities in the Configuration Management process

6.3.2 Roles in the process

Overall responsibility is borne by the **process owner**. The operational tasks of the **process manager** include:

- Maintenance of the definition of all CI and relationship types.
- Schedule regular checks of configuration information in the CMDB.
- Ensure that the verification of configuration information is performed and that the elimination of discrepancies is initiated.

Each CI stored in the CMDB is assigned a **CI owner**. The CI owner ensures that the information stored for the CI is up-to-date and works with the process manager and other CI owners to ensure that all CIs and their relationships are up-to-date.

6.3.3 Requirements

The following requirements are described for this process:

- CONFM 11.1: Define configuration items (CIs) and relationships;
- CONFM 11.2: Define level of detail CI recording;
- CONFM 11.3: Create and maintain CMDB;
- CONFM 11.4: Control CIs and monitor changes;
- CONFM 11.5: Regularly review contents of the CMDB.

CONFM 11.1: Define configuration items (CIs) and relationships

The effective and efficient management of the contents of the CMDB is essentially determined by the information to be entered. For this purpose, the different types of entries must be designed in a meaningful way. This includes defining the CI types and the necessary attributes. The individual CI types are related to each other. The necessary relationships must be represented. The following capability levels are described in FitSM-6.

Capability level	Description
1	The scope of configuration management is intuitively understood and there is awareness of the importance of defining CI types. However, there is neither definitive documentation on the scope, nor a common understanding of the required or permissible CI types and CI relationship types.
2	The scope is documented in a general manner. There is documentation about CI types and relationship types, but it is incomplete, e.g. does not contain all required types or is missing definitions of attributes.
3	The scope and also all CI types and relationship types that can be used in the CMDB are clearly defined and documented. The definition includes CI attributes and, where applicable, relationship attributes as well as allowable combinations of CI types and relationship types. Responsibilities for the maintenance and updating of these definitions are also documented.

CONFM 11.2: Define level of detail CI recording

Like the design of the types of configuration items, the level of detail of the recorded configuration information is an important aspect for the quality of the CMDB and the workload to maintain it. The default must be that the information is sufficient to support effective control over the CIs. The requirements for this come from numerous other FitSM processes.

Capability level	Description
1	Configuration information is only recorded at a very basic level. The information recorded for each configuration item frequently remains unaltered even after the deployment of an extensive change to the CI.
2	The information recorded is generally enough to control each CI. Significant changes are reflected in updated attributes or relationships in the appropriate CI records most of the time. Nevertheless, the level of detail that ends up being recorded in practice is not really planned and defined. For example, attributes might be recorded that are not defined in the CI type definitions and defined attributes might frequently remain unrecorded.
3	There are defined responsibilities and procedures for accurately recording and updating configuration information for all CIs at a planned level of detail. This level of detail is sufficient to document all important aspects of significant changes to CIs and the overall configuration in a transparent and comprehensible manner.

CONFM 11.3: Create and maintain CMDB

IT service providers usually have various databases containing information about their configuration items. In addition to the entries themselves, the relationships between them must be documented. This information is required to support decision making, for example, when assessing a change request. The following capability levels reflect this:

Capability level	Description
1	There is awareness of the concept of a CMDB, but it is implemented in a very basic mode or not implemented at all. The most important configuration information is available from different pieces of documentation, including databases and tools.
2	A CMDB is used to store information on CIs and their mutual relationships are maintained. It is quite comprehensive, but does not yet contain records of all CIs and relationships that contribute to service components and services according to the intended CMDB scope. Different sources of configuration information, including databases and tools, have been partially integrated.
3	A fully integrated CMDB exists, which contains complete records of CIs and relationships according to an adequately defined and documented scope. The CMDB is maintained following established and documented guidelines or procedures with clear responsibilities for maintenance and ownership.

CONFM 11.4: Control CIs and monitor changes

Decisions are made on the basis of the information held in the CMDB. Therefore, an outdated CMDB is useless. Consequently, it is important to ensure that the CMDB is updated when changes are made to the physical and logical IT environment. FitSM-6 formulates the following capability levels for this purpose:

Capability level	Description
1	Changes may or may not be tracked in the CMDB. There is no guarantee that the information recorded for all CIs in the CMDB reflects the current status of such CIs.
2	Changes to CIs are usually reflected in changes to CI records in the CMDB. However, responsibilities and procedures for keeping the CMDB up-to-date with deployed changes are not clearly defined and the data quality varies.
3	The information contained in the CMDB reflects the status and current configuration of all or almost all CIs. There are documented procedures and responsibilities for keeping CMDB information up-to-date during all phases of changes and releases.

CONFM 11.5: Regularly review contents of the CMDB

Even if all changes are tracked in the CMDB, a regular review of the contents is necessary. The goal is to identify possible deviations, i.e. an inventory of the actual IT infrastructure is carried out.

Capability level	Description
1	The information stored in the CMDB is not subject to regular reviews for verification purposes. If, as a consequence of some event, a verification is performed, the respective approach is not specified. The quality of the data stored in the CMDB is not controlled in a reliable fashion.
2	Verifications of the information stored in the CMDB are not planned and scheduled, but they are conducted at somewhat regular intervals. The scope and accuracy of the verification checks varies. All in all, some level of quality control is exerted over the information in the CMDB.
3	The information stored in the CMDB is verified at planned intervals and with a defined scope. Quality of data in the CMDB is kept at a solid level, sufficient to meet the requirements of the other service management processes.

7 Eliminate and Prevent

During the provision of agreed services, disruptions inevitably occur in the use of the services by users and in operations in general. These disruptions must be analyzed and eliminated, especially if contractual agreements from the service level agreements are violated, i.e., promises are not kept. In addition, users often require support in using the services. For example, access to services or user accounts must be set up and general questions about the services answered. The fact that this area has the most intensive contact with the user is of particular importance. For the IT organization, this means that employees working with customers and users need not only technical skills but also excellent interpersonal skills.

The described tasks are divided into the following processes:
- Incident & Service Request Management (ISRM);
- Problem Management (PM).

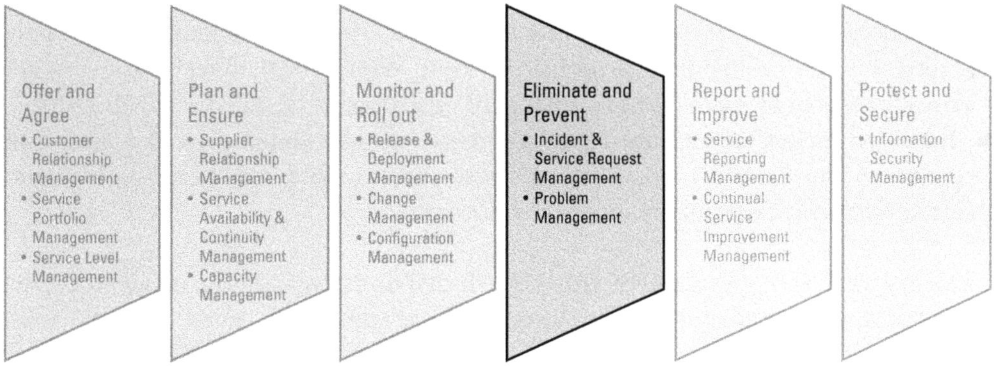

Figure 24: FitSM process model for Eliminate and Prevent

7.1 INCIDENT & SERVICE REQUEST MANAGEMENT

When services are in operation, incidents and service requests occur. The Incident & Service Request Management process resolves incidents and fulfills/responds to service requests. Troubleshooting relates to services for which a service level agreement with specific service targets has usually been agreed. The focus here is on restoring the service as quickly as possible so that it can once again properly support the customer's business processes.

Service requests are requests from users for IT support. A service request does not constitute an interruption of service. In the event of an incident and a service request, the users and, if necessary, the customer must be able to contact IT and process these communications.

7.1.1 Process description

If a service or component does not function as planned, this is referred to as an incident. Incidents usually result in the failure, or a significant reduction in the quality, of a service. When considering whether an event is an incident, it is irrelevant whether a failed component is currently being used by users. An incident remains an incident even if users do not notice it.

Incidents are present in the following cases:

- A service or service component is interrupted or not available.
- The quality of a service falls below a level agreed in the SLA. If the level has not been agreed, we can potentially raise an incident if the quality is below an expected level. In practice, this leaves a great deal of room for interpretation.
- The same applies to service components whose performance levels have been defined in an OLA (internal service provider) or in a UA (external service provider). If the service level is not defined, there is also a corresponding scope for interpretation here.
- The failure of a redundant component is a gray area in FitSM. For example, if a power supply unit fails on a server that continues to run due to two redundant power supply units, this can be handled as part of Incident Management if such cases are not already covered by established maintenance procedures.
- The same applies to the impending failure of a service component. If a hard disk generates unusual noises, it can be declared defective and considered an incident. However, FitSM does not prescribe this procedure.

Incidents are often noticed and reported by affected users. In addition, incidents can be identified through tool-supported monitoring of relevant components.

Not every contact by a user is an incident. If a user requests assistance outside of dealing with an incident, this is referred to as a service request.

Service requests can be very different:

- A request for information, "How can I print double-sided on the new floor printer?"
- A request after a consultation, "Can you tell me if you can do a color graphic like that with our word processor?"

- Commissioning access changes: "A new team member needs access to our project directory."
- Resetting passwords and accounts: "I forgot my password, please reset it." or "After multiple incorrect entries, my user account has been locked. Please reactivate it."
- Commissioning a Standard Change: "A new colleague needs a workstation computer."

When an incident or service request occurs, it goes through a series of activities.

Recording
The most important data is recorded. This includes who reported the incident, who is affected by the incident, which service component is affected, and the specific nature of the incident.

Classification
Incidents and service requests are categorized based on common properties, common relationships or other criteria. Based on the category, an ITSM tool can pick out known solutions or current, Known Errors from a database. If incidents and service requests are to be forwarded to a team with special expertise or specific rights, this team can often be identified by the category. It is also possible to generate statistics on the areas in which more or fewer incidents are occurring.

Prioritization also takes place as part of the classification process.[14] As only limited personnel resources are available, it is not possible for any number of agents to deal with every incident immediately. Incidents and service requests are therefore prioritized according to their relative importance. It is important but often not easy to find objective criteria for determining priority. The most sensible approach is to derive them from specifications in the SLAs.

The situation-specific impact and urgency of an incident or a service request can be used to determine a priority. In the case of impact, criteria such as the number of affected users could play a part, or whether a service is completely down or only slightly impaired. The urgency is usually based on the consequences for the customer's business operations. Various combinations result in this way:

- Impact low, urgency low:
  Example: After an update, a user can no longer print on the central floor printers, but only on his local inkjet printer. This is significantly slower and more expensive. Only one user is affected and the impact on the company's or agency's business operations is likely to be minimal.

14 While ITIL refers to both categorization and prioritization, FitSM combines these into one step called classification.

- Impact high, urgency low:
  Example: An incident on a server means that it currently takes about twice as long as normal to start the workstations. All users are affected, the impact on business operations is high.
- Impact low, urgency high:
  Example: A user's account was locked due to multiple incorrect password entries. This user needs to export reports for an audit. The meeting with the auditors will take place in two hours. If the reports are not available, a new meeting must be arranged. The auditors would charge for the additional effort. The user submits a service request to reset the user account.
- Impact high, urgency high:
  Example: The central parcel control system of a parcel service has failed. Hardly any employees on the evening shift can work anymore, and business operations for loading vehicles are largely at a standstill.

A matrix can then be used to derive the priority from impact and urgency. This example assumes a simple structure. In practice, one should try to act similarly. More priority levels do not necessarily bring more timely processing.

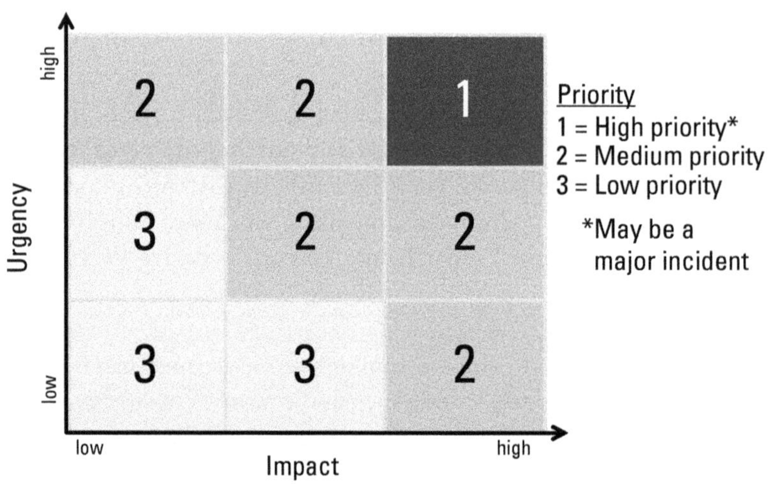

Figure 25: Determination of priority from impact and urgency

In some cases, the customer already wants certain systems to be given priority in the SLA. Many tools can map this automatically by deriving priorities from the previously selected categories. It's also possible to give preferential treatment to certain user groups (VIPs) through the allocation of increased priority levels.

Analysis

The incident is narrowed down and a solution is sought. Various information and tools can support this process:

- A database of Known Errors and corresponding workarounds.
- Current configurations and changes to the configurations.
- Information on currently deployed releases.

Escalation if necessary

The previous activities are usually carried out by a Service Desk, which acts as a single point of contact for users ('first level support'). If the Service Desk is unable to resolve the incident or fulfill the service request, it may make sense or be necessary to call in additional competencies or further specialist knowledge ('second level' or 'third level support'). This process is referred to as escalation.

- Hierarchical escalation:
  If decisions have to be made that go beyond the competencies of the current processing level, the incident is communicated to roles with more extensive authority and accountability. This could be, for example, a chargeable order from a supplier. A rule violation due to a lack of capacity can also be a reason for escalation. For example, a priority one incident that is not resolved within four hours could be automatically escalated hierarchically so that a remediation team is assembled.
- Functional escalation:
  If the expertise or competence required for the solution exceeds that of the employee, further know-how is called-in via functional escalation. This is the case, for example, when the Service Desk cannot resolve a network fault and someone from the network administration department has to take care of it.

Restoration of the service

When a solution has been found and implemented, normal service operation should be restored. An incident can also be resolved via a workaround. The important thing is that the user can work again in accordance with the agreements in the service level agreement. If it is not possible to eliminate an incident and further investigation of the cause is required, the Problem Management process comes into play. This situation is dealt with in the following chapter.

Closure

An incident can be closed when service has been restored; A service request can be closed when it has been properly fulfilled or responded to. It should be defined from the outset what needs to be checked and documented when an incident is closed. In particular, recurring incidents should be identified and appropriate information forwarded to Problem Management, which is responsible for investigating the underlying causes and eliminating any weaknesses.

Additional procedures should be defined for those incidents of such high impact and urgency that normal incident management procedures are inappropriate – so-called 'major incidents'. This refers to situations in which a large part of the essential business processes cannot be executed due to an incident. In manufacturing companies, for example, this can be a production standstill, in logistics service providers it can be the failure of picking or loading control, and in retail companies it can be the web store or order acceptance. Often, such a situation leads to the formation of a special team, along with initiating constant communication with key managers.

If you ask users about their relationship with the Service Desk, the answer is not always satisfactory. Users often have the impression that no one is taking care of their concerns, when in fact they are being actively worked on. This impression can be reduced by keeping users well-informed of progress. A web front-end to the ticket tool is often sufficient for this purpose, allowing users to inquire about the current processing status at any time.

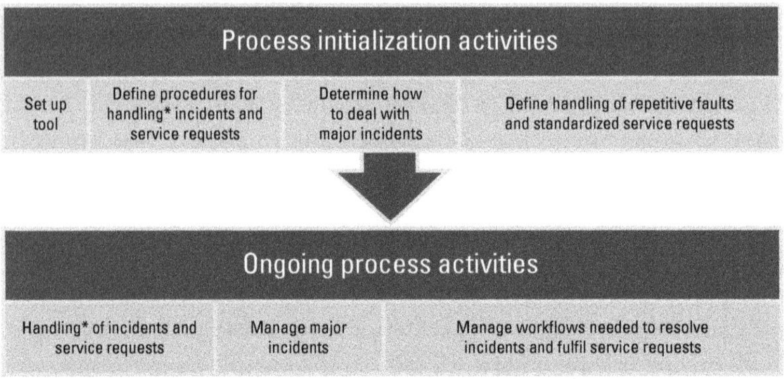

Figure 26: Activities in the Incident & Service Request Management process[15]

7.1.2 Roles in the process

The overall responsibility is borne by the **process owner.** When creating a process description, they should pay particular attention to the interfaces to problems and to Change Management. Furthermore, they need the requirements for their process from the service level agreements.

The operational tasks of the **process manager** appointed by the process owner include:

- Ensure that all incidents and service requests are recorded in sufficient quality so that they are traceable and enable long-term analysis.
- Monitor progress of incidents and service requests and identify potential violations of response and resolution times.

For each incident there is an **incident owner** and for each service request there is a **service request owner.** In their particular case they take care of:

- Coordinating and assuming responsibility for all activities in the lifecycle.
- Progress monitoring and checking whether the processing is still within the specified time frame.

—

15 All activities from recording to closing

- Triggering reminders to stakeholders and escalating to the process manager when necessary.
- Triggering of communication and escalation according to SLA, in the event of SLA violation.
- Ensuring adequate documentation depth.

As specialists, the **process employees** specifically process the fault reports and service requests on the basis of the process description.

7.1.3 Requirements

The process for troubleshooting and handling service requests is described by means of six requirements, of which the first five in particular govern the process:

- ISRM 9.1: Uniformly record, classify and prioritize incidents/service requests;
- ISRM 9.2: Resolve/fulfill incidents/service requests according to SLA specifications;
- ISRM 9.3: Escalate incidents/service requests uniformly;
- ISRM 9.4: Inform customers and users about progress;
- ISRM 9.5: Closing incidents/service requests uniformly;
- ISRM 9.6: Identify and handle major incidents consistently.

ISRM 9.1: Uniformly record, classify and prioritize incidents/service requests

IT must ensure that users' fault reports and service requests are processed. The first step is to ensure that all user cases are documented. Handwritten records can be lost, have limited availability and are not sufficiently structured for further process control. This requirement can only be met by introducing a tool for electronic documentation. In addition to the recording itself, a classification must be carried out, which on the one hand can be used for later evaluations and process optimizations, and on the other hand controls the further processing of this case (processing department/specialists, schedule, prioritization, . . .).

Capability level	Description
1	Not all incidents and service requests are registered; some are handled without the creation of any record. Existing incident records vary significantly in format and level of detail. Determination of priorities is often not consistent.
2	Most incidents and service requests are recorded, classified and prioritized. Criteria for prioritization and classification are not documented. They are done in an intuitive way, but by and large lead to consistent results.
3	All incidents and service requests are registered and then classified and prioritized according to defined and documented criteria. Prioritization criteria are designed based on an understanding of service targets.

ISRM 9.2: Resolve/fulfill incidents/service requests according to SLA specifications

Service targets are agreed and defined with the customer in the SLAs. These also concern the prioritization of incoming messages from users. This ensures that there is a uniform and documented understanding of the order of processing. The following capability levels are described in FitSM for this purpose:

Capability level	Description
1	Incidents are resolved and service requests fulfilled on a case-by-case basis. Records of resolved incidents and service requests vary in terms of the quality of documentation, which is often incomplete.
2	Incidents and service requests are handled according to established procedures. The interfaces to Service Level Management and Problem Management are not documented, but documentation on SLAs and Known Errors is used repeatedly. Records are generally complete, although the level of detail and style of documentation varies.
3	All incidents are resolved, and all service requests are fulfilled. Service Level Management and Problem Management interfaces are defined, information from SLAs and about Known Errors is taken into account when handling incidents and service requests. Records are complete and information is recorded in a consistent manner that allows the status to be tracked.

ISRM 9.3: Escalate incidents/service requests uniformly

The escalation of incidents and service requests is an important and often necessary activity in daily operations. It ensures that incidents and service requests are processed on time and helps the person responsible for the case or the process employee to obtain the necessary support. The following capability levels are documented:

Capability level	Description
1	Based on the situation and individuals involved, incidents and service requests may be escalated. There is no pre-defined escalation path to follow. Incidents and service requests sometimes stay 'stuck' or unresolved for a long time.
2	Incidents and service requests requiring IT are functionally or hierarchically escalated in the majority of cases. While there is an intuitive understanding about the escalation path to follow, it remains undefined and there are no, or only few, defined triggers or documented responsibilities.
3	Incidents and service requests are escalated when required based on documented responsibilities and procedures. Triggers and guidance for functional and hierarchical escalation exist and are used to decide how to handle incidents and service requests. This results in consistent behavior in escalation of incidents.

ISRM 9.4: Inform customers and users about progress

Communication with users is an activity the importance of which is not always understood by IT employees. It helps the acceptance of IT's work enormously if, for example, the progress of reported incidents and triggered service requests are continuously accessible and a message is triggered when important events occur. FitSM-6 provides for the following capability levels:

Capability level	Description
1	There is some communication with users regarding their incidents and service requests. This is done at the discretion of individual members of the support staff.
2	Users and customers are informed of the progress of their reported incidents and service requests. This includes both responding to customer and user status requests as well as proactive notifications. However, there is no clearly defined and systematic approach for this type of customer communication and responsibilities are not documented.
3	Users and customers are systematically informed of the progress of their reported incidents and service requests. This happens both in a reactive and proactive way, according to a defined approach and documented responsibilities for support staff.

ISRM 9.5: Closing incidents/service requests uniformly

As soon as incidents have been resolved and service requests have been processed, the case must be closed in a uniform manner. Closure procedures regulate which conditions must be met in order to set a final status, whether the user must give his or her consent, whether final checks or even post-documentation are carried out, and how the quality of the documentation is evaluated. The capability levels are described in FitSM-6 as follows:

Capability level	Description
1	Incidents and service requests are closed based on individual choice by support staff, after they are resolved or fulfilled, or for other reasons (such as remaining unresolved for too long). There is no consensus approach for when incidents should be closed or what other actions should be taken.
2	Incidents and service requests are closed in a generally consistent way, and for appropriate reasons. Appropriate other actions are also taken when incidents and service requests are closed. However, there is no documented approach and responsibility for this activity.
3	Incidents and service requests are closed in a consistent way according to documented guidelines or procedures and responsibilities. Other actions, such as confirmation of closure with users, are taken when appropriate.

ISRM 9.6: Identify and handle major incidents consistently

In order to be prepared for incidents with extremely far-reaching significance, clear definitions must exist for identifying these major incidents and for dealing with them in a uniform manner. This means, for example, an organizational policy for the composition of corresponding teams and a definition of when such an incident becomes a major incident.

Capability level	Description
1	There is some idea of which incidents should be regarded as 'major'. In these cases, special care and attention is given to the respective incidents, but how they are handled remains inconsistent.
2	There is an understanding about which kinds of incidents should be regarded as major incidents. Major incidents are classified and named as such, and special care and attention is given to them, including handling them with the highest priority, coordination through a sufficiently senior level of management, communication and post resolution review. However, responsibilities and clear definitions of major incidents are not documented.
3	There is a clearly defined and understood approach for the classification and management of major incidents from occurrence to closure, including effective communication, coordination of resolution activities and post resolution review. There is a documented set of criteria for major incidents, and responsibilities are also documented.

7.2 PROBLEM MANAGEMENT

Problem Management determines the causes of incidents and creates sustainable solutions. In this way, recurring incidents can be avoided or the impact of existing incidents can be minimized. Workarounds allow users to get back to work before a permanent solution is implemented. Such workarounds are also developed in Problem Management and made available to Incident Management.[16]

A problem is the (as yet unknown) underlying cause of one or more incidents that require closer investigation. While Incident Management focuses on the users and tries to ensure that they can get back to work as quickly as possible (rapid troubleshooting), Problem Management pursues the sustainable stabilization of the service environment (root cause analysis).

7.2.1 Process description

An incident can frequently be investigated and resolved based on the resolution of previous incidents and the further know-how of those involved. In contrast, a problem requires a specific root cause analysis.

One of the tasks of Problem Management is to analyze incidents and identify potential problems. The following situations should lead to a documented problem:

- An incident occurs repeatedly. Even if service can be quickly restored each time, for example by a restart, a permanent solution should ensure that the frequency with which this incident occurs can be reduced. It may even be possible to eliminate the cause completely.

—

16 This does not exclude the fact that (especially simple) workarounds are also identified and applied in the Incident & Service Request Management process without Problem Management being involved.

- One or more incidents occur and cannot be resolved without detailed root cause analysis.
- An evaluation of historical incidents uncovers previously unrecognized failure patterns, indicating that a systemic problem may exist. This suggests an increase in fault tolerance.

The underlying cause of several incidents is analyzed via a problem and, ideally, permanently eliminated. However, if there is only a single incident, a corresponding problem does not necessarily have to be created for the root cause analysis. The aim behind this is to avoid unnecessarily increasing the level of administration in such situations.

In the case of very high reliability requirements, it may be useful to go beyond the requirements defined by FitSM and consider proactive problem management. This involves stabilizing the components relevant to service provision even though no incidents have yet occurred. Such a case exists if, for example, components exhibit unexpected behavior, or entries in log files indicate unusual behavior. There does not have to be an incident yet, but symptoms are observed that could potentially lead to incidents. In this case a problem entry can also be created to get to the bottom of the cause.

Process steps
Problem entries are classified for later evaluation. Just like incidents, they are assigned to a category. In addition, a priority is assigned in the same way as for Incident Management. This determines how quickly work must be done on the problem.
The cause is now identified as part of the root cause analysis. In parallel, a workaround is sought. Sometimes it is important to already know the cause in order to find a workaround, though this is not always the case. For example, a restart can restore functionality even without knowing the cause. A workaround has the advantage that users can get back to work before a final solution has been implemented. However, a workaround may cause additional work for the user and may not deliver the promised performance of the service. But important functionality is available again, while the final solution is still waiting due to insufficient resources, non-existent skills or other reasons.

As soon as a documented workaround is available, or even a temporary workaround, the problem is given the status Known Error[17]. The cause has not yet been eliminated at this point. By applying the documented workaround, negative effects on the services can be minimized or even eliminated while work continues on the root cause analysis and sustainable elimination.

After a solution has been found that eliminates the cause of the problem, it can be implemented. Once the solution has been successfully implemented, the problem entry

17 In FitSM, the cause does not necessarily have to be known in order for a problem to receive Known Error status. It is sufficient if only a workaround exists. This is where FitSM differs from some other ITSM frameworks, where knowledge of the cause is explicitly required as a prerequisite for a Known Error.

is closed. If changes have to be made to a configuration item when implementing the solution, the solution is implemented by Change Management as part of a change. The task of Problem Management is then to submit a corresponding change request.

Change Management is not obliged to approve the change request. A rejection could be justified, for example, by the fact that the effort is disproportionate to the benefit. In such a case, the problem (with Known Error status) is not eliminated. The workaround becomes a permanent solution.

It may happen that during the investigation of the problem, i.e. during the root cause analysis and the search for a workaround, a permanent solution is found right away. If the implementation effort and time of the permanent solution does not exceed that of the workaround, the permanent solution is implemented immediately. In this case, the problem entry can be closed without ever documenting the Known Error status. This is to avoid unnecessary administrative effort in FitSM.

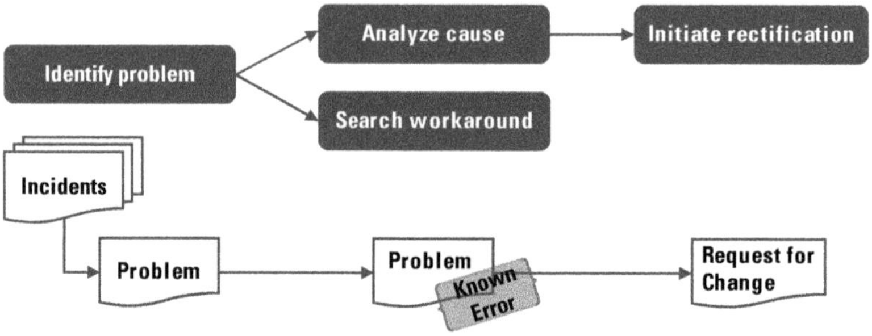

Figure 27: Example of the Problem Management process

A practical example to illustrate this

In Incident Management, one or more users report that an application is taking an extremely long time to complete certain transactions. This often ends in a termination. In the last few weeks, this has happened again and again. Corresponding incidents are created. These remain open as long as the application displays this behavior. In the context of Problem Management, a problem entry is created and linked to the corresponding incidents. In this way, it is clear that the issue is currently being worked on. The problem entry is assigned a category that most likely matches the category of the recorded incidents. Priority is determined by defining urgency and impact. The root cause analysis begins. It quickly becomes apparent that since an update a month ago, the log files are no longer archived and emptied daily as usual. The manufacturer of the software had transferred this function to an additional module to be installed with the update. The log files occupied more and more space on the hard disk, which meant that there was no longer enough room for temporary files of the application.

As a workaround, the log files are archived and emptied manually. After a restart, the application reacts as expected again. This workaround is documented, giving the problem entry the status Known Error. The users can work again and the incidents in the Incident & Service Request Management process can be closed.

In the Problem Management process, a solution is worked out that permanently eliminates the cause: Installing the software module for archiving the log files, according to the manufacturer's instructions.

The solution is submitted as a change request to the Change Management process. There it is assessed and approved. Since the software module to be implemented reorganizes the database and makes far-reaching changes to the overall package, the implementation is handed over to the Release & Deployment Management process.

After testing and installing the software module on the target system, a check is made to see whether the conversion was successful (PIR). After a successful check, the problem entry can be closed. If there are still open incidents linked to the problem at this point, these can now also be closed. In this example, however, all incidents could already be closed with the workaround.

A Known Error Database (KEDB)

The database used to manage problem and know error records throughout their lifecycle is called the KEDB. In practice the KEDB is usually part of the same system that is used to track incident and service request records. In this way, records can easily be linked to each other to ensure efficient and effective ticket activity.

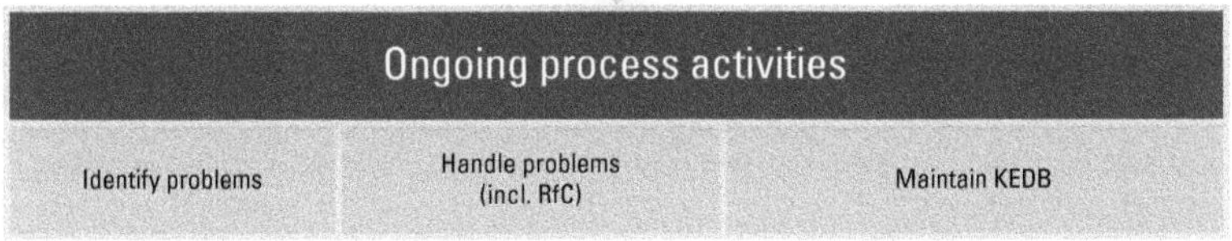

Figure 28: Activities in the Problem Management process

7.2.2 Roles in the process

The **process owner** has the overall responsibility for the process and, in particular, must define the interfaces to the Incident & Service Request Management processes. The **process manager** assumes the following tasks:

- Setting up a tool for process support.
- Ensure trends in incidents are analyzed regularly to identify issues.

- Ensure that identified problems are recorded with sufficient quality.
- Ensure issues are analyzed, information on Known Errors is recorded, and issues are brought to closure.

Each problem is assigned a **problem owner,** who is responsible for the specific problem:
- Coordination and responsibility for all activities in the lifecycle.
- Monitor progress and ensure escalation occurs as needed.
- Ensure that information related to the specific problem, including descriptions of potential workarounds, is documented in an up-to-date manner.
- Communication of the problem/Known Error and potential workarounds to relevant stakeholders (for example, Service Desk and users).
- Trigger a change request or Continual Service Improvement process, depending on the solution options selected.

7.2.3 Requirements

The following requirements are formulated for Problem Management:
- PM 10.1: Identify problems consistently;
- PM 10.2: Investigate and solve problems;
- PM 10.3: Record Known Errors;
- PM 10.4: Maintain current information on Known Errors.

PM 10.1: Identify problems consistently

One of the main tasks of Problem Management is analyzing the cause of existing incidents. This must be done in a structured manner, i.e., regularly and uniformly in a procedure. It is therefore important to translate the need for ongoing incident analysis and elimination into a methodical approach. In FitSM-6, the capability levels are described as follows:

Capability level	Description
1	If and how a problem is identified and registered depends on the individuals involved. Significant effort sometimes goes into resolving problems that are never identified and registered as such.
2	There is a common understanding of when and how problems should be identified and registered. Incident records are routinely investigated to identify unrecorded problems with significant impact.
3	There is a defined and documented approach for the identification and registration of problems. This includes provisions as to when and by whom incident records should be analyzed on a regular basis.

PM 10.2: Investigate and solve problems

Once the problems have been identified, they must be investigated in more detail to identify the cause. Then the problems are eliminated through suitable measures. To this end, organizational arrangements must be made to ensure that a goal-oriented treatment is carried out. One outcome should also be to identify and reduce the impact on services if the problem cannot be rectified immediately.

Capability level	Description
1	If a problem has been identified, it is investigated on an individual basis, depending on the person or group feeling responsible for it.
2	If a problem has been identified, further investigation follows a well-understood sequence of actions. However, this approach and the roles involved have not, or have only partially, been defined and documented.
3	A formal approach to investigating identified problems is in place. Roles and responsibilities are documented. The approach covers the general actions to be carried out to resolve the problem or reduce its adverse impact, such as identifying potential problem resolutions and workarounds and assessing their cost-benefit ratio.

PM 10.3: Record Known Errors

Until a problem can be permanently eliminated, a workaround should be identified and documented. If the problem cannot be permanently eliminated, a workaround is necessary to restore service when incidents occur. The problem entry is assigned the status of a Known Error. The documentation is an important source for Incident & Service Request Management in troubleshooting and often shortens the time required to resolve related incidents.

Capability level	Description
1	Which actions are taken after the root cause of a problem is identified varies and depends on the individuals involved.
2	There is a common, if undocumented understanding that, if an immediate problem resolution is not practicable even after the identification of the root cause, an effort should be made to reduce the impact through workarounds.
3	Trying to identify actions to eliminate or reduce the impact of the problem after its root cause has been identified is part of an established and well-defined approach. In the event that the problem cannot be resolved, or resolution would be inefficient, the problem is classified as a Known Error and the respective workaround is documented in a Known Error database using a uniform format for its description.

PM 10.4: Maintain current information on Known Errors

The problems dealt with must be documented in an appropriate system to ensure easy searching and quick retrieval of the workaround. This Known Error database should be seen as an important working tool (a database) in which not only the company's own Known Errors are documented, but also those reported by suppliers. The following capability levels are distinguished in FitSM:

Capability level	Description
1	Information on Known Errors and their workarounds is maintained in varying locations and varying formats. Personnel involved in the Incident & Service Request Management process are sometimes not aware of updates to this information and do not always have access to it. Responsibilities for maintaining the information and making it available are not clearly understood.
2	Information on Known Errors and their workarounds is usually kept up-to-date, though this is not universally perceived as the responsibility of Problem Management. Updated information is made available to personnel involved in Incident & Service Request Management through well-known but undocumented channels.
3	There is a defined and established approach, including guidelines and/or procedures, for maintaining information on Known Errors and their workarounds and making it available to staff involved in the Incident & Service Request Management process.

8 Report and Improve

For both customers and users, it is important to know whether the agreed service has been provided at the defined quality (service targets). The users of the services and other responsible parties usually only have a subjective assessment of this. An effective, efficient reporting system linked to the service objectives ensures a reliable, factual basis for determining service results. To this end, reporting should not be based solely on the technical components and the IT infrastructure. It must be determined whether the performance (the service) is also being received by the corresponding users. Service providers can also report on their performance and document the quality of their work. Often, service failures and negative experiences are the focus in the evaluation of the work. This can be countered with a coordinated reporting system. In addition to reporting on the quality of service provision, a structured approach is required to continuously improve the company's own processes and results. This can be reflected, for example, in higher quality or lower effort in the provision of services. The target is to provide service in a cost effective way, so quality and costs needs to be balanced.

The reporting and improvement area basically comprises the following statements:

- Reporting and improvement based on the type of reporting outlined above are fundamental elements of a healthy service management system, and reporting provides objective data to enable fact-based decision-making.
- Through sound reporting, organizations can evaluate the degree to which SLAs, OLAs and UAs are being complied with, understand the quality and performance of both services and processes, identify opportunities for improvement, and support communication regarding activity, quality and performance with all stakeholder communities.
- While it is valuable to have the facts, simply possessing the knowledge is not enough. It must be acted upon. Continual improvement is based on information gleaned from reporting and the success of improvement efforts is validated through reporting.

Continual improvement is based, among other things, on reporting and is a central element of FitSM. In the general requirements GR 4-GR 7, continual improvement is manifested using the PDCA cycle. This general approach must be transferred to the operational work which is done by a process.

To map the tasks of reporting and continual improvement in this way, FitSM describes two processes:

- Service Reporting Management (SRM);
- Continual Service Improvement Management (CSI).

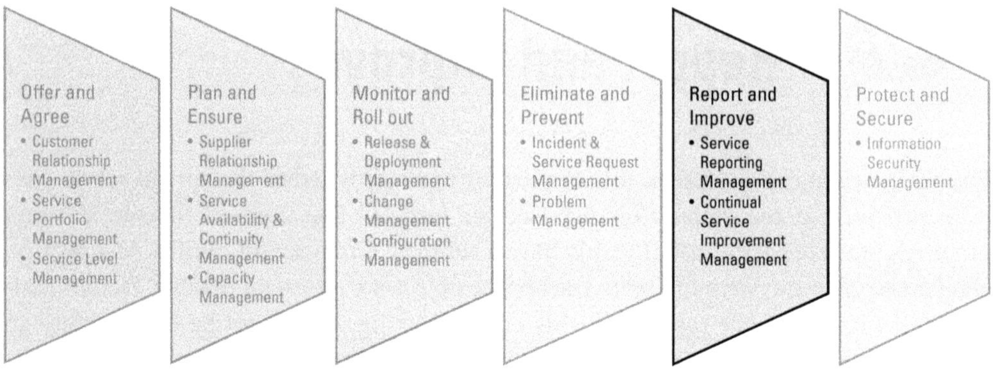

Figure 29: FitSM process model for Report and Improve

8.1 SERVICE REPORTING MANAGEMENT

The objective of Service Reporting Management is to specify reports on services and processes and ensure they are produced and delivered. In this context, a 'report' means traditional reports on paper, or as a PDF document. In addition to this more static variant, it also refers to the provision of dashboards that are made available online and allow the recipient to interact with the data. It is therefore a process that helps all other processes and all process/service owners to create and deliver adequate reports. Adequate means that reports are aligned with the requirements of the report recipients. In the same way that fault processing or capacity planning are made more professional through process description, the establishment of roles and the implementation of requirements, so the focus of professionalization is also on reporting and thus on communication about the company's own performance.

8.1.1 Process description

Service targets were defined with customers in the SLAs. To determine whether these targets have been met, the relevant components and the overall service results must be subjected to regular measurement. End-to-end results may be difficult to measure, but that doesn't mean the attempt should not be made. This can involve, for example, the response times of an application, its availability, or the speed of fault elimination. The measurement results are compared with the agreed targets and summarized in a report tailored to the target audience. In addition to the degree of target achievement, other aspects can also play a role in reporting. The number of changes carried out shows the activities that a service provider undertakes to keep the service components constantly up-to-date. In the case of an online store, for example, a report on user behavior could be of significant interest. A report for the customer, therefore, typically contains the parameters agreed in the SLA.

A report for internal use can also contain aspects from the OLAs. In this way, it is possible to check the extent to which the availability of database servers, for example, meets the expected (agreed) specifications. To check the agreements with external suppliers, measurement criteria can be taken from the UAs, e.g., bandwidth utilization. In this case, the values for reporting can be determined by the company itself or communicated by the external service provider.

In addition to the consideration of services, processes must also be subjected to measurement and reporting to evaluate how well they are performing against their goals. For example, a process goal could be to improve the throughput time of incidents or changes. Reports are a valuable tool, especially regarding the continual improvement of processes. The recipients of these reports are the process and service owners and the SMS manager.

Reports generally serve to record a factual situation in order to derive decisions from it. It is therefore important to prepare reports in a way that is appropriate for the target audience. A report for management is usually condensed and limited to important key values, while a report for an operational team tends to have more detailed values. Depending on the target audience, descriptions of measures that have been initiated, are still in progress, or have already been successfully completed may also be useful.

It can be useful to standardize and automate the reports. This facilitates their creation and increases the recognition value for all target audiences. A reliable, standardized structure enables customers, management or administrators, for example, to quickly find the data relevant to themselves.

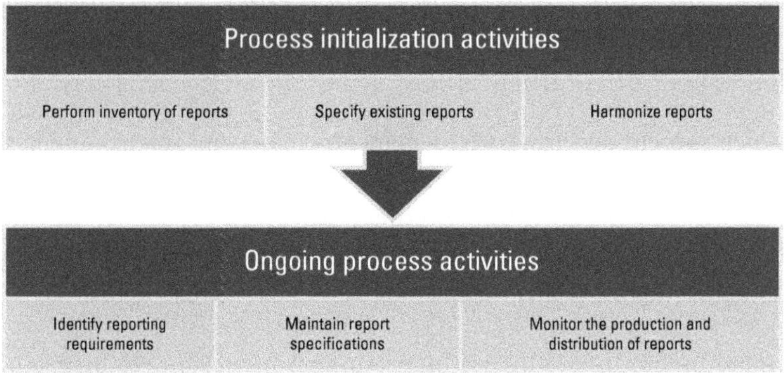

Figure 30: Activities in the Service Reporting Management process

8.1.2 Roles in the process

In this process, once again, responsibility for target definition, documentation, and resource provision lies with the **process owner**. Among other things, the process owner should determine how the reporting requirements from the SLA, OLA, and UA documents of the Service Portfolio Management process are communicated to Service Reporting Management. Furthermore, they must be aware of the process targets that are provided to them by the respective process owners and managers.

The operational tasks of the **process manager** include in particular:

- Create a list of reports and keep it up-to-date.
- Regularly check the specifications of the reports.
- Monitor regular reporting in accordance with the requirements.

For each **report** there is a **responsible person (owner)** who ensures the following:

- Maintenance of the specifications for the respective report.
- Preparation and provision of the report according to the specifications.
- The data required for reporting is available in a timely manner.
- Observance of new or changed requirements for the specifications of the report.

8.1.3 Requirements

For service reporting, three requirements are described in FitSM:

- SRM 3.1: Identify reports;
- SRM 3.2: Specify reports;
- SRM 3.3: Create and distribute reports.

SRM 3.1: Identify reports

Systems, IT infrastructure components or applications are frequently used to deliver a whole range of reports as standard. In order to steer this diversity in an orderly manner and ensure effective use, clear identification must be made. For this purpose, performance must be presented in comparison with agreed targets from the SLA, OLA and UA agreements. Furthermore, information about important events (such as security or major incidents, far-reaching or failed changes) and identified cases of non-conformance (process deviations) must be included.

The task is therefore not to present one's own performance via a mass of reports and key figures, but rather to build up and standardize targeted reporting. This applies equally to reports on processes. Reports must support the derivation of measures as well as succinctly enabling readers of the reports to assess service or process quality. FitSM-6 summarizes this in the following capability levels:

Capability level	Description
1	Recipients can receive some reports on demand. Required reports have not been identified for the entire SMS. Service reports do not cover all the relevant information (performance against targets, events and nonconformities).
2	Most required reports have been identified, but on a largely informal basis. Responsibility for reporting is not clearly documented.
3	All required reports have been identified. Reporting covers performance of services and processes against defined targets, significant events and detected nonconformities.

SRM 3.2: Specify reports

To adequately align the reports with the needs of the recipients, important elements must be generally defined in advance of their creation. These include:

- A clear designation of the report (sequential numbering or concise, meaningful name);
- Its purpose (why is this report being created, what question should it answer?);
- Its audience (management, business, IT internal, . . .);
- Its frequency (weekly, monthly, . . .);
- Its content (affected services, components, or users);
- Its format (dashboard, paper, graphs included, textual supplement, . . .);
- The method of delivering the report (sending via email, delivering in a portal, handing over with personal explanation, . . .).

The capability levels look as follows:

Capability level	Description
1	Although there is a general awareness about what needs to be reported to whom, and at what intervals, most reports have not been specified.
2	Most reports are specified and have been agreed with their recipients, including customers, but on a largely informal basis. General information on identity, purpose, audience, frequency, content and method of delivery may be provided, but it is not documented in a clear or systematic way. While reports are produced, responsibilities are not always clear.
3	Reports are agreed with their recipients, including customers, and are delivered based on documented responsibilities. All reports are specified in a systematic way, covering identity, purpose, audience, frequency, content and method of delivery for each report. Every report has a clearly defined owner.

SRM 3.3: Create and distribute reports

This requirement focuses on the need to produce and deliver reports to their intended recipients in accordance with specified criteria and the method of delivering the report (e.g. sending via email, delivering in a portal, handing over with personal explanation, . . .). Nowadays many reports are available in systems as on-demand and are available at all the times. Organizations must follow defined specifications to create reports that meet the required format, content, and delivery timelines. This includes collecting and analyzing relevant data, generating accurate and comprehensive reports, and ensuring their timely distribution to the designated recipients. By adhering to the specified requirements, organizations can provide valuable insights, updates, and information to stakeholders in a consistent and reliable manner. This ensures effective communication, facilitates decision-making processes, and enables stakeholders to stay informed and make informed decisions based on the information presented in the reports. The capability levels look as follows:

Capability level	Description
1	Recipients can receive some reports on demand; others are produced at irregular or unspecified frequencies. Reports do not cover all relevant specifications.
2	Reports are regularly produced, but they do not always meet all specifications. Report formats are not consistent, and may differ significantly, e.g. between reports for different services or groups of services.
3	Reports are produced and delivered to recipients on a regular basis in a specified and consistent format. Reports contain all necessary specifications.

8.2 CONTINUAL SERVICE IMPROVEMENT MANAGEMENT

The task of the Continual Service Improvement Management process is to identify opportunities for improvement, prioritize them, plan and support their implementation, and to monitor their execution. This process considers both services and processes. It is thus the operational extension of the service management system and the PDCA cycle. It provides valuable support for top management (see Chapter 3 General requirements) and ensures continual improvement within the SMS.

8.2.1 Process description

On one hand, the process activities focus on the service management system, i.e., the implementation of the specifications from top management in the ITSM processes. On the other hand, continual improvement focuses on the services provided by the service provider.

With regards to the service management system, the focus is on the basic organization as well as the individual processes and their activities. As far as the focus on the services is concerned, it means concentrating on the individual services and their service components. Since there is a very close dependency between service and process quality, the two areas cannot be considered completely separately.

When improving the service management system, the level of compliance, effectiveness and efficiency is optimized.

A **conformance test** examines the extent to which the service management system implements the general requirements, and the individual processes implement the process-specific requirements from FitSM-1. If an organization has defined more extensive requirements for the processes in the service management system, compliance with these organization-specific requirements can also be checked as part of a conformance test. It is also possible to check compliance with external requirements, such as customer or legal requirements. In practice, one also speaks of compliance with regards to the observance of such specifications. If a deviation is detected, this is referred to as a nonconformity.

A review of **effectiveness** determines the degree of goal achievement and examines whether the activities carried out are suitable for achieving the goals set. This is also referred to as the effectiveness of the activities. The following questions, for example, can be asked as part of an effectiveness review of Problem Management:
1. Are the individual activities effective in preventing recurring incidents?
2. Can a reduction in incidents be measured or verified since the introduction of these activities?

Thus, while a compliance audit examines compliance with requirements, an effectiveness audit indicates the extent to which these requirements are suitable for achieving the objectives.

Efficiency in this context pertains to economic viability, where the effort expended in activities should align meaningfully with the benefits gained. It's crucial to assess both effectiveness, which measures the success of activities, and efficiency, which gauges cost-effectiveness simultaneously. For instance, while increasing personnel in Problem Management may reduce recurring incidents, the question of efficiency arises: does the cost incurred justify the reduction in incidents?

Service improvement optimizes the quality or performance of an entire service as well as individual service components. The quality and performance targets are usually derived from customer requirements. Analogous to the processes, effectiveness and efficiency are also reviewed here.

Before starting an improvement, the desired goals must be identified. To do this, it makes sense to ask which factors are critical for the success of a process or a service. In the case of a service, these critical success factors include the targets agreed with a customer in the SLA. The question then arises as to how the achievement of objectives can be measured in a meaningful way. Key performance indicators (KPIs) are derived for this purpose, which also clearly define how a specific issue is measured. One such critical success factor of Change Management could be the stability of the infrastructure, in that implemented changes deliver their planned benefits and do not result in any disruptions. The ratio between unsuccessful changes and the total number of changes could serve as a performance indicator.

Identified opportunities for improvement should be recorded and prioritized. It is advisable to give preference to simple changes with a high benefit value during implementation (quick wins). In the case of complex changes, not only the benefits and costs but also the expected burden on the organization must be considered closely. Only after a positive assessment is made can a schedule be drawn up and Continual Service Improvement Management give the go-ahead.

If a change to a configuration item is required for improvement, the Continual Service Improvement Management process generates a request for change in the Change Management process.

Within the framework of continual improvement, it must be determined which objects are to be subjected to an audit and at what intervals, and which aspects are to be audited.

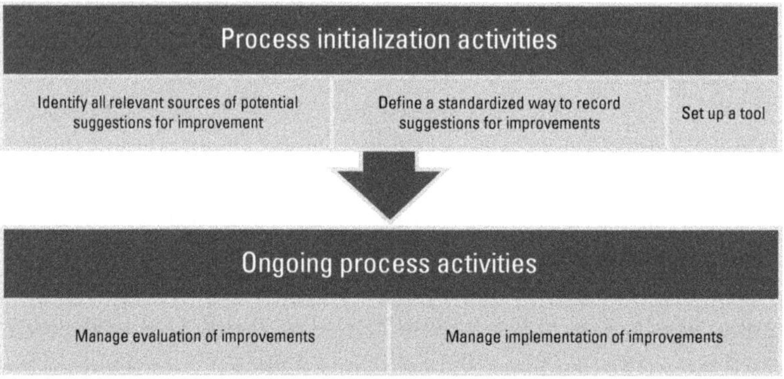

Figure 31: Activities in the Continual Service Improvement Management process

8.2.2 Roles in the process

The **process owner** bears overall responsibility and provides the necessary resources, while the **process manager** implements the operational tasks of the process. This includes regularly checking the status and progress of ongoing improvements. Due to the relationship of the process to top management and the resulting requirements, overlaps in operational work may occur. It therefore makes sense to consider whether top management should assume at least one of these two roles.

For each identified improvement, there is an **improvement owner** who coordinates the activities to implement an improvement and controls the implementation. These activities can be of a more technical nature or focus on process-related issues. In terms of scope, they can tend to be smaller changes or have a project character that is more long-term and extensive.

8.2.3 Requirements

Three specific requirements are formulated for the Continual Service Improvement process:

- CSI 14.1: Identify potential for improvement and plan audits;
- CSI 14.2: Evaluate and implement potential improvements in a uniform manner;
- CSI 14.3: Monitor implementation of improvement measures.

In addition, numerous general requirements, for example from the PDCA cycle, are also entrusted with Continual Service Improvement (see Chapter 3 General requirements).

CSI 14.1: Identify potential for improvement and plan audits

This requirement addresses the importance of identifying and registering opportunities for improvement in services and processes. Organizations must actively seek out areas where enhancements can be made by analyzing reports and utilizing results from measurements, assessments, and audits of the service management system (SMS). By systematically evaluating the efficiency and effectiveness of the SMS, organizations can identify areas of potential improvement and capture these opportunities for further action. This proactive approach enables organizations to continuously enhance their services and processes, address any shortcomings or inefficiencies, and drive ongoing improvement and optimization within the service management framework. The capability levels are described as follows:

Capability level	Description
1	Opportunities for improvement are recognized largely by individuals somewhat randomly and registered in a haphazard manner, if at all.
2	There is some common approach for seeking improvements and recording them that is carried out on an ongoing basis. However, opportunities are not identified systematically, and not all are registered. Responsibilities are undocumented.
3	There is a clearly defined approach to identifying and recording opportunities for improvement of services and processes that is enacted on an ongoing basis. It is based on reports, results from measurements, assessments and audits of the SMS.

CSI 14.2: Evaluate and implement potential improvements in a uniform manner

Based on identified opportunities, this requirement underlines the need for consistent evaluation of opportunities for improvement and the identification of appropriate actions to address them. Organizations must establish a systematic approach for evaluating potential areas of improvement, ensuring that a consistent and objective assessment is applied across different opportunities. By doing so, organizations can effectively prioritize and select the most impactful improvement actions to undertake. This evaluation process should reflect various factors such as feasibility, impact on service quality, resource requirements, and alignment with organizational goals. Once the opportunities for improvement have been evaluated, organizations can then identify specific actions and initiatives that will address these areas and drive positive change within the organization. This approach fosters a culture of continual improvement and enables organizations to proactively enhance their services and processes. In FitSM-6, the following capability levels are described for this purpose:

Capability level	Description
1	When opportunities for improvement arise, there is a person or group responsible for deciding how to proceed, generally a member of management rather than a group or individual with specific responsibility for improvement. Decisions are more likely based on the opinion or knowledge of the person or group taking the decision than a defined set of criteria.
2	There is some commonly understood approach to evaluating and approving opportunities for improvement, based on a set of criteria. The approach is broadly followed, though not all roles and responsibilities are defined, nor decisions and actions to address them always clearly recorded.
3	The approach for evaluation and approval of opportunities for improvement is clearly defined. It is carried out whenever new opportunities have been identified, based on defined roles and responsibilities. It is based on clearly identified criteria that seek to maximize the effectiveness of the SMS and related capabilities of delivering services according to customer needs and agreed SLAs. Actions to address the identified opportunities for improvement are recorded.

CSI 14.3: Monitor implementation of improvement measures

Once improvement activities have been approved and implemented, monitoring should begin. On the one hand, it is a matter of monitoring the activities themselves and, on the other hand, ensuring that the objectives are achieved. Improvement activities are at risk of being forgotten in an operational rush. Consequently, organizations that understand the benefits of continual improvement make sure that these precise activities are prioritized accordingly. The true and above all sustainable success of ideas for improvement only comes to fruition when these ideas are implemented. However, it is important to note that activities which have not been completed, or have even failed, can provide insights. A 'failure' can therefore provide a positive contribution to continual improvement. The capability levels look as follows:

Capability level	Description
1	Implementation of actions for improvement is done on a case-by-case basis.
2	Improvement actions are usually implemented, but this implementation is not always documented. Some improvement measures remain unimplemented for a considerable length of time.
3	The implementation of improvement actions is consistently managed, their status is monitored and their effectiveness reviewed upon completion.

9 Protect and Secure

Where information is processed, its security also must be ensured. This is not just about protection against malicious attacks and fierce competitors. In recent years, a steady increase in legal requirements has also been observed[18] .

By identifying risks and dealing with them appropriately, an adequate level of security can be created at a reasonable cost. FitSM describes the steps required for this in the Information Security Management (ISM) process.

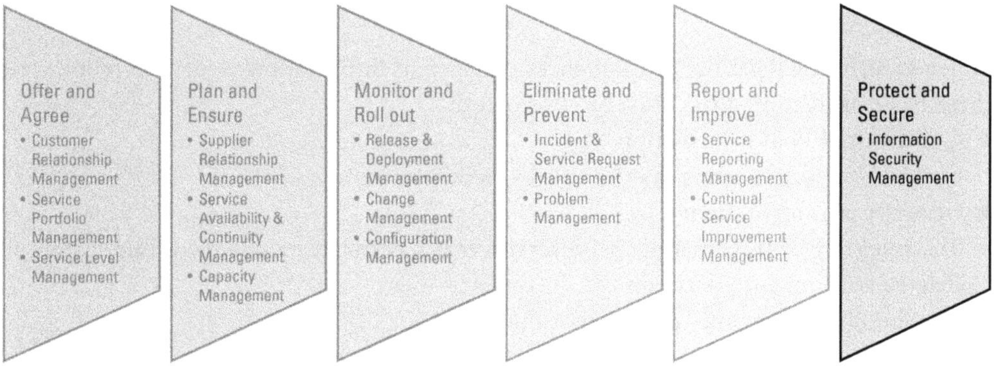

Figure 32: FitSM process model for Protect and Secure

9.1 INFORMATION SECURITY MANAGEMENT

Information Security Management involves identifying the necessary level of information security, i.e., confidentiality, integrity, and availability/accessibility of information, and ensuring this level is achieved and maintained across all service delivery activities.

—

18 Examples of legal requirements for information security: Federal Data Protection Act, IT Security Act, KonTraG, GoBD, Sarbanes-Oxley Act.

9.1.1 Process description

The first step in achieving an adequate level of security is to identify the information security requirements. It is necessary to determine what level of information security is required, i.e., what level of protection do data and information require? In this process, so-called information assets are identified. *Information assets* represent the information and information processing systems that are of value to an organization. The term 'value' should not be interpreted too narrowly. For all existing information that is not identified as an information asset, i.e. that does not represent value for the organization, the question should be posed as to why this information is not destroyed.

With the increasing shift of systems and applications to the cloud, more and more cloud services can be found in the asset directory.

When determining the need for protection, it helps to create a classification scheme. The German Federal Office for Information Security (BSI) suggests three protection requirement categories:

- Normal: The damage impact is limited and manageable.
- High: The damage impact can be significant.
- Very high: The damage impact can reach an existentially threatening, catastrophic level.

When identifying what the consequences of a lack of information security might be, all three basic protection goals must be considered:

- Confidentiality of information:
  Only authorized persons may be able to view information.
- Integrity of information:
  The integrity of information is preserved if it has not been changed, duplicated or deleted without authorization.
- Availability/accessibility of information:
  Information can be accessed and used by authorized persons.

Information security is often first associated with confidentiality. However, this view does not cover all aspects. For example, generally accessible data on a website has a low level of confidentiality. However, it can be important to protect it against unauthorized modification. Customer requirements for information security should already be specified in the SLA.

Once the required security level has been identified, the risks that could jeopardize this level must be established. This could be an automated attack from the Internet, a phishing e-mail, a virus or a targeted attack from outside or inside the company. However, accidental deletion of important information by employees is also a possibility. The aim is to reduce the probability of potential risks occurring and to minimize their potential impact should they actually occur. A mix of different information security controls is used to counteract the identified risks by reducing their probability of occurrence and/or impact. The measures can be broadly divided into three areas:

- Technical measures, such as virus scanners, firewalls or technical restrictions on password length.
- Organizational measures, such as guidelines for handling external data carriers, or requirements for locking the workstation when leaving it unattended.
- Measures to increase awareness that serve to make employees aware of the consequences their actions can have. This aspect is often underestimated in practice, even though employees' mistakes due to ignorance and carelessness are among the most frequent causes of damage.

The ISO/IEC 27001 standard describes specifications for setting up an Information Security Management system. The aim is to determine the necessary information security requirements and to achieve and maintain an adequate level of security. This standard includes an annex in which measures are listed. This list provides a useful overview of the various aspects that need to be considered when defining measures. They concretize the description from FitSM very effectively and are therefore used here.

Guidelines can help to achieve and maintain the desired level of security. Examples of such guidelines are:

- Overarching information security policy;
- Specific safety guidelines for certain systems or areas;
- Password policy;
- Email policy;
- Mobile device usage policy;
- Access control policy;
- Guideline for the disposal of media;
- Vulnerability management policy.

This list is not exhaustive, but merely reflects the most important, basic documents. Guidelines should be formulated as simply and comprehensibly as possible. They should restrict the target audience in their work activities only to the extent that is absolutely necessary. If new guidelines prohibit previously practiced procedures for business-relevant activities, alternatives may have to be offered.

The threat situation of an organization is constantly changing. Attackers develop new attack methods, new technologies bring new threat potential, economic success moves a company into the focus of competitors. For this reason, identified risks should be checked at planned intervals to ensure that they are up-to-date. The more changeable the environment of an organization, the closer the intervals of such a review should be.

In addition to the actuality of the risks, the effectiveness of the derived measures must also be tested. Many technical measures can be tested by so-called penetration tests, i.e., simulated attacks. In the case of organizational measures, it can happen that technology develops further but the guidelines are not adapted in line with this. Formulations such as "DVDs are to be disposed of as follows. . ." should be adapted as part of a review. Part of reviewing awareness measures is determining whether employees are aware of the relevant policies and are complying with them, because policies that only look good on paper do not increase information security.

Events that potentially compromise information security can occur at any time. Some of these information security events are predictable, such as an employee receiving a phishing email, while others may not have been anticipated. If an information security event is likely to have a negative impact on the customer's service delivery or business activity, it is called an information security incident. It is important to establish a procedure for handling information security incidents in order to counter them with appropriate measures in a reasonable time.

For users to be able to work, they need access to information processing systems and services that they are authorized to use. The use of individual functions or modules as well as access to information within the systems and services is controlled via more detailed access rights. Information Security Management determines how authorized users obtain the access and access rights they need, while at the same time keeping unauthorized users out of the loop. This also includes the regulation of how the granted rights can be subsequently revoked. This does not mean that making every access change is an activity of this process. Rather, ISM makes the security specifications to which the other processes must adhere. The individual user access requests are handled as service requests in the Incident & Service Request Management process.

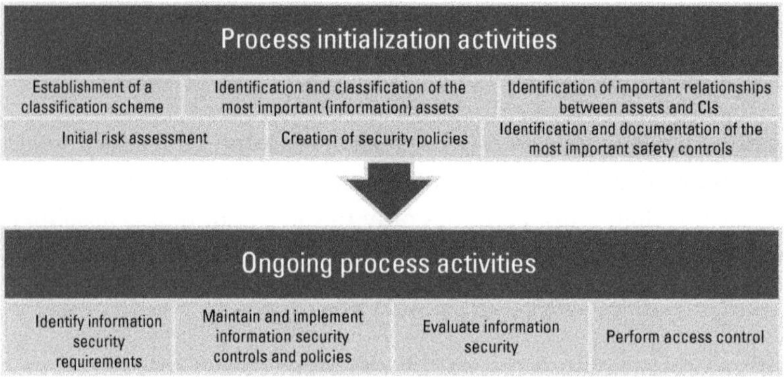

Figure 33: Activities in the Information Security Management process

9.1.2 Roles in the process

The **process owner** has overall responsibility and appoints the **process manager**, who is often called the ISO (Information Security Officer) or CISO (Chief Information Security Officer) internationally.

The operational responsibilities of this role include:

- Primary contact for all information security issues.
- Monitoring the status and progress of all process-related activities, especially a sensitive information inventory, information security risk assessment, handling of security-related events and incidents.
- Ensuring that information security incidents are identified, classified, and addressed as quickly as possible to minimize the damage they may cause.
- Ensuring that all safety-related documents are kept up-to-date.

An **information security risk manager** handles the following tasks:

- Ensuring the completeness and timeliness of an inventory of sensitive information.
- Ensuring that data owners maintain descriptions and classifications of their data and provide information needed to identify security risks.
- Regularly performing a risk assessment, based on available information about the data to be protected and current information about vulnerabilities and threats.

For the most important information worth protecting, there is one owner of the data **(asset owner)** in each case. This means that the asset owner is familiar with the data and the data requirements. In addition, the asset owner should be familiar with legal requirements and relevant agreements, for example with third parties. Since they also know how the data is integrated into business processes, they are in a position to determine which persons or groups of persons have read or changed access to this data. They can determine the consequences of a violation of a basic value of information security (confidentiality, integrity, availability/accessibility) with regards to their data stock, and they determine the protection requirement. The need for protection in turn determines the required level of security, which is then reflected in the appropriate security measures.

The main tasks of this role are:

- Maintaining and reviewing the description and classification of sensitive data in a directory.
- Acting as primary contact for questions about the data to be protected.
- Assisting in identifying and analyzing information security risks related to the data to be protected.

For each security measure, FitSM-3 recognizes an **information security control owner**. They have the following tasks:

- Managing and reviewing the specification/documentation covering the information security measure.
- Acting as primary contact for questions about the specific security measure.

9.1.3 Requirements

To achieve information security, five requirements are placed on the Information Security Management process:

- ISM 6.1: Define information security (IS) policies;
- ISM 6.2: Assess IS risks regularly;
- ISM 6.3: Implement IS measures;
- ISM 6.4: Handle IS events/incidents consistently;
- ISM 6.5: Implement access control in a consistent manner.

ISM 6.1: Define information security (IS) policies

As described earlier, guidelines help to achieve and maintain the desired level of safety. FitSM-6 describes the following capability levels for this purpose:

Capability level	Description
1	The service provider is aware that information security policies are important to achieve a solid level of awareness and overall direction in maintaining a sufficient level of information security. Some policies exist, but many of them are followed by intuition rather than being formally documented and approved.
2	There is a general consensus on information security requirements, even if they are not fully documented. Documented information security policies are established and address predominantly technological issues.
3	Information security requirements are established and regularly reviewed for appropriateness, e.g. when the context of the organization or technology changes. Information security policies are established and govern technological, physical, people-related and organizational issues. Responsibilities for maintaining, developing and auditing compliance with the policies are documented.

ISM 6.2: Assess IS risks regularly

Content for this requirement has already been described above. Various information security measures are required to counter the identified risks. The following capability levels are described specifically in FitSM:

Capability level	Description
1	Some information security risks are identified, but the assessment of these risks is irregular and does not follow the same approach for the whole organization. The results of risk assessments are often not easily comparable with each other.
2	Information security risks are identified. The results of reasonably regular assessments follow a largely uniform structure (e.g. use the same number of levels for determining probability and impact). However, more detailed procedures are not documented. If assessments are carried out by different persons, the results are not always directly comparable.
3	Information security risks are identified in a planned manner and with standardized tools (e.g. hazard/threat catalogs). Risks are assessed using clearly defined criteria and procedures that allow for the comparability of results.

ISM 6.3: Implement IS measures

As has already been described, the threat situation is constantly changing. Therefore, a corresponding review of the various guidelines and measures is also necessary.

Capability level	Description
1	The service provider is aware of the need for controls to maintain and enhance information security. Some controls are in place. However, they are often undocumented.
2	Information security controls including measures to support operations and communication security as well as physical and environmental security are in place, and there is a clear understanding of who is responsible for which controls. Most controls are documented, though documentation approaches may differ between different types of controls.
3	For all information security topics relevant to the service provider, information security controls have been defined and implemented. The controls reduce the probability and impact of identified information security risks and meet identified requirements. Controls cover technological, physical, people-related and organizational issues. Owners have been defined for all information security controls and their responsibilities documented. All information security controls are linked to related risks and assets.

ISM 6.4: Handle IS events/incidents consistently

This requirement establishes the link to Incident Management. Security-relevant events and incidents must be recorded and processed as incidents. If there are corresponding regulations in the SLA, these must be implemented. If this is not the case, the service provider must still be aware of the relevance of these incidents. The capability levels are as follows:

Capability level	Description
1	The service provider is aware that information security incidents may have a significant impact on the customers and on the service provider's capabilities to deliver agreed services to customers. It is understood that an effective response to any information security incident is essential. If an information security incident is identified, it is managed to the best of knowledge, but without a structured and defined approach being followed.
2	Information security events are monitored on an ongoing basis to identify potential information security incidents. If an information security incident is identified, the response to this incident follows a consistent and well-understood sequence of actions. However, this approach and the roles involved have not, or have only partially been defined and documented.
3	A formal approach to monitoring information security events and dealing with information security incidents is in place. Roles and responsibilities are documented. The approach covers well-defined criteria for classifying an event or situation as an information security incident, the actions to be carried out to analyze the security incident and reduce its adverse impact, and the associated communication and documentation.

ISM 6.5: Implement access control in a consistent manner

Based on the protection requirements of the existing information assets (information and information processing systems), a consistent set of methods for regulating access authorizations and access control must be developed. FitSM formulates the following capability levels for this purpose:

Capability level	Description
1	Access rights for information processing systems and services are provided on an individual basis, with no clear access control policies being in place.
2	The provision of access rights follows a combination of intuitive rules and some defined policies, which support a mostly consistent approach to access control. From time to time, access rights are reviewed.
3	Access control, including the provision, review and revocation of access rights, follows a structured and defined approach with clear policies and procedures.

10 Federated IT infrastructures

Traditional IT service management models assume that there is a single IT service provider that exercises sole central control over its IT service management processes. In practice, this traditional form is the most common variant. However, in many situations IT services are also provided jointly by several service providers as part of a federation. In this case, IT service management processes must be implemented or coordinated across organizational boundaries.

The environment from which FitSM originally emerged consisted of a large number of organizations operating data centers and other technical and non-technical sites throughout Europe, and which, based on a federated infrastructure, jointly provided various IT services to their (also distributed) customers. In such federations, responsibilities and competencies for processes are distributed among several organizations. Roles in processes are assumed by people from different organizations. When designing FitSM, care was taken not to make any assumptions that would prevent or complicate its use in such an environment. This is especially true for the requirements from FitSM-1, which are also suitable for collaborative models in service delivery.

From the perspective of IT service management in federated environments, it is important to understand what type of federation is present in a specific case and what requirements result from this for the design of the service management system, its processes and roles. The FitSM standard does not provide a specific taxonomy for classifying different federation types. However, there are certain 'extreme cases' between which a federation can move:

- Invisible coordination: This case is characterized by the fact that the customers of the services clearly perceive the individual federation members as such and obtain their services directly from them. If a customer purchases multiple services from different service providers in the federation, they also conclude multiple SLAs with these providers. The federation is merely created by the fact that there is some form of coordination or cooperation in service delivery between the providers that is not or barely perceived by the customer. As a result, each service provider probably establishes its own IT service management processes, and rather selectively, processes or parts of them are federated.

- Fullservice integration: At the other end of the scale, customers perceive the entire federation as a single (virtual) service provider. The individual federation members remain hidden, or are irrelevant. Here there is a great need for overarching and federation-wide IT service management processes, such as a common Service Portfolio Management, which ensures uniform SLAs with all customers across all services in the common service catalog.

Between these models, various intermediate stages are conceivable. Ultimately, it is critical to understand how providers will work together in a collaborative model, where this will result in services for customers, and how the processes for managing these services will be designed and coordinated between members of the federation. As a basis for this, the organizational structure underlying the service delivery must be identified, including a possible federation structure, as well as the contact points and contacts for all parties involved. This is also a requirement in Service Portfolio Management (PR1.4).

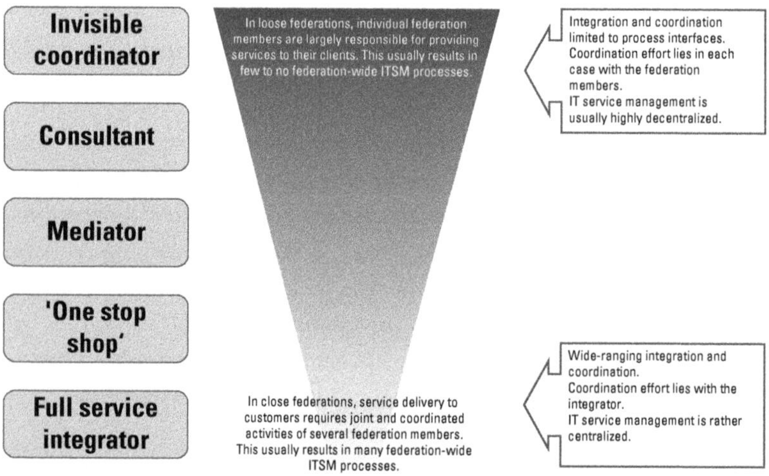

Figure 34: Possible structures in federations

The federated idea in IT service management is becoming more and more established in practice, even in commercial enterprises. The demands on an internal IT department or an IT service provider are growing faster or greater than can be satisfied by what the single organization alone can provide. Regulating cooperation via contracts is often associated with the desire for agreement and control. This view is gradually being replaced by trust-based cooperation between several IT service providers with the goal of a satisfied customer. The federative idea of FitSM is very helpful here.

Summary and outlook

This FitSM book seeks to provide a comprehensive guide to establishing a lean and efficient IT service management (ITSM) framework for small and medium-sized enterprises. We first covered the history, target audience, and motivation behind FitSM, as well as its basic concepts and terms. We then delved into the general requirements of FitSM, including documenting the service management system, creating process descriptions, documenting process results, and managing documentation. The book also discusses the PDCA (Plan-Do-Check-Act) cycle as a continual improvement methodology that is central to FitSM.

We have explained all of the FitSM processes in Chapters 4 to 9. Each chapter describes the processes related to a superordinate value stream step. Each chapter also outlines the process descriptions, roles, and requirements for each of these service management processes. Overall, this FitSM book provides a practical and comprehensive guide to implementing a lightweight ITSM framework that can benefit IT managers and service providers of all sizes.

The book also emphasizes how the strength of the FitSM approach lies in its focus on the specific requirements that organizations need to address for an effective IT service management system, rather than getting bogged down in excessive detail. The book stresses the importance of a 'continual improvement' mindset, where organizations can make small, incremental improvements to their service management practices over time. This aspect is dealt with more intensively and in greater detail in the second book.

A key aspect of the practical implementation of FitSM is the 'maturity assessment' that provides a reference point for continual improvement. By assessing their current capabilities against the FitSM requirements, organizations can identify areas to focus on and make targeted improvements, rather than trying to overhaul their entire service management system at once. This aspect is presented in context in the second book and illustrated using two example companies.

Overall, this book presents a promising, lightweight approach to IT service management that is well-suited for organizations of small and medium sizes looking to improve their service delivery in a practical and continual manner. The key will be effectively translating the FitSM requirements into real-world, people-centric improvements. This book presents the theoretical aspect of IT service management and FitSM in detail, while the second book describes the practical implementation and provides real life examples.

Appendix A: FitSM personal certification

FitSM offers the possibility for individuals to demonstrate a certain level of knowledge via a personal certificate. There are a total of four exams, which build on each other at three levels. The syllabus on which these exams are based was developed by the FitSM working group and has proven itself in practice since the beginning. On the one hand, it makes it easy to get started and, on the other, it offers more in-depth training content.

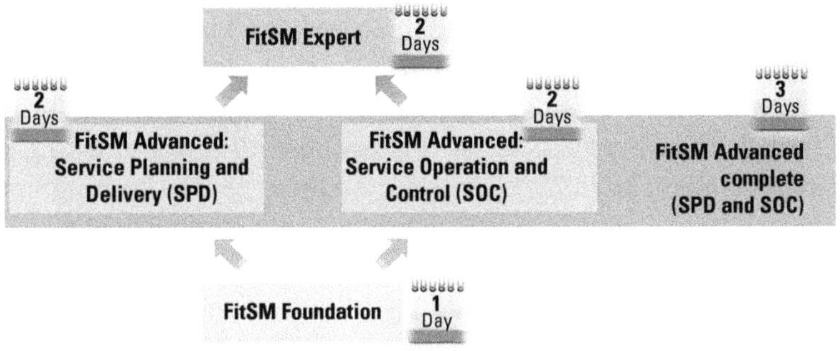

Figure 35: Qualification scheme of FitSM

The **Foundation level** is represented by the exam "Foundation in IT Service Management". It certifies basic knowledge in IT service management and is of interest to all persons who come into direct contact with the processes. This does not have to be limited to IT employees, and can also be useful for customers, facility management or purchasing professionals. A seminar preparing for this exam lasts one day. To take this exam, a seminar must be attended at an accredited training provider. The website fitsm.online offers further information and accredited online training for the Foundation Level including the certification exam by APMG.

At the **Advanced level,** there are two possible exams, which are primarily aimed at people who will design and implement processes or take on responsible roles within a process. There are separate two-day preparatory seminars for each of the two exams. A successful pass in the Foundation certificate is a prerequisite for taking an Advanced exam. Some training providers also offer combined three-day training for both exams.

The syllabus and the training content allow and support this. For the FitSM Advanced Level, the website fitsm.online also offers further information and accredited online training including the certification exam by APMG.

The "Service Planning and Delivery" exam looks in particular at the processes that provide services on the basis of customer requirements. The "Service Operation and Control" exam focuses on processes that serve the operation of services and the associated support and control.

At the **Expert level,** the FitSM personal certification concludes with the "Expert in IT Service Management" examination. This covers the implementation of a service management system as well as continuous quality assurance and is aimed at IT management, persons with a mandate to implement a service management system and persons who would like to work as consultants in the area of FitSM. A prerequisite for admission to this exam is successful completion of both Advanced Certificates.

The content of this book addresses both the Foundation and Advanced exams for FitSM certification. It provides comprehensive coverage of the essential concepts and practices required for both levels, ensuring readers are well-prepared for their certification journey. The Foundation level content establishes a solid base of knowledge in IT service management principles, while the Advanced material delves deeper into practical implementation and strategic aspects of FitSM. By addressing both levels in a single volume, this book offers a seamless learning experience, allowing readers to progress from foundational understanding to advanced proficiency in FitSM methodologies.

The task of conducting examinations and accrediting training institutes has been delegated to APMG International by the FitSM rights holder ITEMO worldwide. The training institutes accredited by APMG offer seminars and exams according to the ITEMO regulations. These ITEMO regulations and the provision of the official training materials on the FitSM website ensure that all relevant topics are covered within a seminar. APMG itself offers online examinations in addition to the examinations following the respective seminars. This offer can be used by training participants to allow some time for preparation after undertaking a training course.

Appendix B: Further information and sources

Websites of the authors:
Anselm Rohrer, https://rohrer.info
Dierk Söllner, https://dierksoellner.de

Online training and information:
https://fitsm.online

FitSM official website:
http://fitsm.eu

IT Education Management Organization e.V.:
Owner of the FitSM rights
https://www.itemo.org

itSMF International:
User organization on IT service management topics
https://www.itsmfi.org

International Organization for Standardization:
Holder of the right to ISO standards
https://www.iso.org

AXELOS:
Holder of the rights to ITIL https://www.axelos.com

Federal Office for Information Security, BSI:
Holder of the rights to IT-Grundschutz https://www.bsi.bund.de

Information Systems Audit and Control Association, ISACA:
Rights holder to COBIT
https://www.isaca.org

CMMI Institute LLC:
Owner of the rights to CMMI
https://cmmiinstitute.com/

CORDIS, Community Research and Development Information Service Information on EU project number 312851 "FedSM – Service Management in Federated e-Infrastructures"
https://cordis.europa.eu/project/rcn/104760_de.html

Appendix C: Terms and definitions

For the purpose of the FitSM family of standards, the following terms and definitions apply (source: FitSM-0):

Activity	Set of actions carried out within a process.
Assessment	Set of actions to evaluate the capability level of a process or the overall maturity level of a management system.
Audit	Systematic, independent and documented process for obtaining audit evidence and evaluating it objectively to determine the extent to which the audit criteria are fulfilled. Note 1: Audit evidence is typically based on documented information, information provided during an audit interview, and information gathered through observation. Note 2: Audit criteria may be based on requirements from a management system (including policies, processes and procedures), agreements (including service level agreements and underpinning agreements), contracts, standards or legislation. Note 3: An audit may be an internal audit, if it is conducted under the direct responsibility of the organization or federation that is subject to the audit, or an external audit, if it is conducted by an external party. Note 4: Both internal and external audits should be conducted by skilled and experienced auditors, and auditors should not audit their own work or areas of responsibilities to ensure the impartiality of the results.
Availability	Ability of a service or service component to fulfil its intended function at a specific time or over a specific period of time.
Availability of information	Property of information being available to and usable by an authorized party. Note: Availability of information may also be referred to as accessibility of information.
Capability level	Achieved level of effectiveness of an individual process or general aspect of management.
Capacity	Maximum extent to which a certain element of the infrastructure (such as a configuration item) can be used. Note: This might mean the total disk capacity or network bandwidth. It could also be the maximum transaction throughput of a system.
Change	Alteration (such as addition, removal, modification, replacement) of a configuration item (CI) or another entity that requires change control.

Classification	Assignment of items to defined groups based on common attributes, relations or other criteria Note 1: Items that are subject to classification may include documents, records (such as incident records or change records), services, configuration items (CIs), etc. Defined groups may include categories (such as incident categories or change categories) or priority levels. Note 2: The act of classification often comprises the application of more than one classification scheme. For instance, an incident record might be assigned to a technical incident category such as 'software related', 'network related', etc., and also to a priority level like 'low priority', 'medium priority', etc. The assignment of various incidents, service requests, changes and problems to an affected CI is also a classification. Note 3: Besides the presentation and analysis of relationships, classification is often used as input for controlling the workflow of a process, e.g. by assigning a priority level to an incident.
Closure	Final activity in a workflow of a process to indicate no further action is required for a specific case. Note: Cases that are subject to closure may include incidents, problems, service requests or changes. The activity of closure puts the connected record (such as the incident record, problem record, service request record or change record) in its final status, usually called 'closed'.
Competence	Sum of knowledge, skills and experience that an individual or group needs to effectively take on a specific role.
Confidentiality of information	Property of information not being accessible to unauthorized parties.
Configuration	State of a specified set of attributes, relationships and other relevant properties of one or more configuration items (CIs). Note: The documented configuration of a number of CIs at a given point in time is called a configuration baseline, which is usually taken prior to the deployment of one or more changes to these CIs in the live environment.
Configuration item (CI)	Element that contributes to the delivery of one or more services or service components, therefore requiring control of its configuration. Note 1: CIs can vary widely, from technical components (e.g. computer hardware, network components, software) to non-technical items such as documents (e.g. service level agreements, manuals, license documentation). Note 2: The data necessary for effective control of a CI is stored in a CI record. In addition to attributes of the CI, the CI record likely includes information on relationships it has with other CIs, service components and services. CI records are stored in a configuration management database (CMDB).
Configuration management database (CMDB)	Store for data about configuration items (CIs). Note: A CMDB is not necessarily a single database covering all configuration items (CIs). It may rather be composed of multiple data stores.
Conformity	Extent to which requirements are met in some context. Note: In the context of FitSM, the term 'compliance' is generally used as a synonym for conformity. However, sometimes conformity is used in the context of adherence to internal regulations and requirements as defined by policies, processes and procedures, while compliance is used in the context of adherence to external requirements, such as laws, standards and contracts.
Continuity	Property of a service to maintain all or parts of its functionality, even in exceptional circumstances. Note: Exceptional circumstances include emergencies, crises or disasters which affect the ability to provide services over extended periods of time.

Customer	Organization or part of an organization that commissions a service provider in order to receive one or more services. Note: A customer usually represents a number of users.
Demand	Potential or identified desire of customers for a service.
Document	Information and its supporting medium. Note: Examples of documents include policies, plans, process descriptions, procedures, service level agreements, contracts or records of activities performed.
Effectiveness	Extent to which goals and expectations are met. Note: In a management system, effectiveness is mostly measured against the defined goals of the processes that are subject to this system.
Efficiency	Degree of ability to meet goals and expectations with minimum consumption of resources. Note 1: In a management system, efficiency is mostly considered in the context of the processes that are subject to this system. Note 2: Resources may be human, technical, informational or financial.
Emergency change	Change with a very high urgency to being implemented in order to avoid negative consequences.
Escalation	Change of responsibility for a case (such as an incident, service request, problem or change) or activity to another individual or group. Note: There are two basic types of escalation: Hierarchical escalation transfers responsibility (temporarily) to someone with a higher level of authority. Functional escalation transfers responsibility to someone with a different set of competencies or privileges required to handle the case or activity.
Federation	Situation in which multiple parties, the federation members, jointly contribute to the delivery of services to customers without being organized in a strict hierarchical setup or supply chain.
Federation member	Individual, organization or body that works together with other federation members in a federation to provide one or more services Note: Often, federation members will not be bound together by strict contractual agreements.
Federator	Body that acts to coordinate a set of federation members.
Improvement	Action or set of actions carried out to increase the level of conformity, effectiveness or efficiency of a management system, process or activity, or to increase the quality or performance of a service or service component. Note: An improvement is usually implemented after an opportunity for improvement has been identified, for instance during a service review, audit or management review.
Incident	Unplanned disruption of operation in a service or service component, or degradation of service quality versus the expected or agreed service level or operational level according to service level agreements (SLAs), operational level agreements (OLAs) and underpinning agreements (UAs).
Information security	Preservation of confidentiality, integrity and availability of information.
Information security control	Means of controlling or treating one or more risks to information security.
Information security event	Occurrence or previously unknown situation indicating a possible breach of information security. Note: An occurrence or situation is considered a potential breach of information security if it may lead to a negative impact on the confidentiality, integrity and/or availability of information of one or more information assets.

Information security incident	Single information security event or a series of information security events with a significant probability of having a negative impact on the delivery of services to customers, and therefore on the customers' business operations.
Integrity of information	Property of information not being subject to unauthorized modification, duplication or deletion.
IT service	Service that is enabled by the use of information technology (IT).
IT service management (ITSM)	Entirety of activities performed by an IT service provider to plan, deliver, operate and control IT services offered to customers Note: The activities carried out in the ITSM context should be directed by policies and structured and organized by processes and supporting procedures.
Key performance indicator (KPI)	Metric that is used to track the performance, effectiveness or efficiency of a service or process. Note: KPIs are generally important metrics that will be aligned to critical success factors and important goals. KPIs are therefore a subset of all possible metrics, intended to allow for monitoring a service or process.
Known error	Problem which has not (yet) been resolved, but for which there are documented workarounds or measures to reduce or prevent negative impact on services.
Major change	Change that (may) have a significant impact on one or more services.
Major incident	Incident that (may) have significant impact on the customer.
Management review	Periodic evaluation of the suitability, maturity and efficiency of the entire management system by its accountable owner(s), from which opportunities for improvement are identified and follow-up actions are determined. Note: The accountable owner of a management system is usually a top management representative of the organization operating the management system. In a federation, the accountable owner is usually one person nominated by top management representatives of all organizations (i.e. federation members) involved.
Management system	Entirety of policies, processes, procedures and related resources and capabilities aiming at effectively performing management tasks in a given context and for a given subject. Note 1: A management system is generally intangible. It is based on the idea of a systematic, structured and process-oriented way of managing. Note 2: While documentation (such as process definitions, procedures and records) and tools (such as workflow support and monitoring tools) can be parts of a management system, management system considerations are not limited to the questions of documentation and tool support. Note 3: With respect to (IT) service management and the FitSM standard series, the idea of a service management system (SMS) is a central concept, where the context of the management system is the organizational context of the service provider, and the subject is to plan, deliver, operate and control (IT) services.
Maturity level	Achieved overall effectiveness of a service management system, based on the combination of the capability levels of its processes and general aspects of management.
Nonconformity	Case or situation where a requirement is not fulfilled. Note: This may also be referred to as noncompliance.
Operational level agreement (OLA)	Documented agreement between a service provider and an internal supplier that specifies the underpinning service(s) or service component(s) to be provided by the internal supplier or federation member, together with the related service targets. Note: In a federation, OLAs may be agreed between the federator and federation members.

Operational target	Reference/target value for a parameter used to measure the performance of a service component, listed in an operational level agreement (OLA) or underpinning agreement (UA) related to this service component. Note: Typical operational targets might include availability or allowed resolution times for incidents.
Policy	Documented set of intentions, expectations, goals, rules and requirements, often formally expressed by top management representatives in an organization or federation. Note: Policies are then realized in processes, which are in turn made up of activities that people carry out according to defined procedures.
Post implementation review (PIR)	Review after the implementation of a change that determines if the change was successful. Note: Depending on the specific type and complexity of the change, the post implementation review may vary widely in its depth.
Priority	Relative importance of a target, object or activity. Note: Often incidents, service requests, problems and changes are given a priority status. In the case of incidents and problems, priority is usually based on the specific impact and urgency of the situation.
Problem	Underlying cause of one or more incidents that requires further investigation to prevent incidents from recurring or reduce the negative impact on services.
Procedure	Specified set of steps or instructions to be carried out by an individual or group to perform one or more activities of a process.
Process	Structured set of activities, with clearly defined responsibilities, that bring about a specific objective or set of results from a set of defined inputs. Note: Generally, a process consists of a number of activities used to manage services, if the process is part of a service management system (SMS).
Record	Documentation of an event or of the results of performing a process or activity.
Release	Set of one or more changes that are grouped together and deployed as a logical unit.
Release and deployment strategy	Approach taken to manage releases and their deployment for a given set of service components and related configuration items (CIs), including organizational and technical aspects of planning, building, testing, evaluating, accepting and deploying releases. Note: Typical release and deployment strategies include continuous integration (a DevOps practice where changes to software source code are regularly merged into a central repository, followed by running automated builds and tests) and fixed release cycles (where minor and major releases are planned according to a long-term schedule, with emergency releases being deployed between release cycles as necessary).
Report	A structured record communicating results gathered through measurement, monitoring, assessment, audit or observation. Note 1: A common report generated from a service management system is a service report targeted to customers of a service that details the performance of that service versus the service targets defined in a service level agreement (SLA). Note 2: The recipients of reports may be internal or external, including customers, suppliers, federation members, service owners and the SMS owner.
Request for change (RFC)	Documented proposal for a change.

Risk	Possible negative occurrence that would have a negative impact on the service provider's ability to deliver agreed services to customers, or that would decrease the value generated through some service Note: Risk is made up of the probability of the threat entailed, the vulnerability to that threat of some asset, and the impact the threat would have, if it occurred.
Role	Set of responsibilities and connected behaviors or actions collected into a logical unit that can be assigned to an individual or group. Note: An individual may hold multiple roles.
Service	Way to provide value to customers through bringing about results that they want to achieve. Note: In the context of the FitSM standard series, when referring to services, usually IT services are meant.
Service acceptance criteria	Criteria that must be fulfilled by the time a new or changed service is deployed and made available to customers/users. Note: Service acceptance criteria are defined when a new or changed service is designed, and they may be updated or refined during the development or transition phase. They may cover functional and non-functional aspects of the specific service to be deployed.
Service catalog	Customer-facing list of all live services offered along with relevant information about these services. Note 1: A service catalog can be regarded as a filtered version of, and customers' view on, the service portfolio. Note 2: Based on one service portfolio, one or more service catalogs can be created.
Service component	Logical part of a service that provides a function enabling or enhancing a service. Note 1: A service is usually composed of several service components. Note 2: A service component is usually built from one or more configuration items (CIs). Note 3: Although a service component underlies one or more services, it usually does not create value for a customer alone and is therefore not a service by itself.
Service level agreement (SLA)	Documented agreement between a customer and service provider that specifies the service to be provided and the service targets that define how it will be provided.
Service lifecycle	The series of phases a service may move through in its lifetime. Note 1: Specific service lifecycle phases are typically defined for each organization, depending on the complexity needed. These may include initial idea, proposal, design, development, deployment, production and retirement. Note 2: Service design and transition plans, sometimes referred to as the service design and transition package (SDTP), should be produced or updated for every new or majorly altered service. It may consist of a number of documented plans and other relevant information including a list of requirements and service acceptance criteria, a project plan, communication and training plans, technical plans and specifications, resource plans, development and deployment schedules/timetables, etc.
Service management	Entirety of activities performed by a service provider to plan, deliver, operate and control services offered to customers. Note 1: The activities carried out in the service management context should be directed by policies, and structured and organized by processes and supporting procedures. Note 2: In the context of the FitSM standard series, when referring to service management, usually IT service management is meant.
Service management plan	Overall plan for implementing and operating a service management system (SMS).

Service management system (SMS)	Overall management system that controls and supports management of services within an organization or federation. Note: The SMS can be regarded as the entirety of interconnected policies, processes, procedures, roles, agreements, plans, related resources and other elements needed and used by a service provider to effectively manage the delivery of services to customers.
Service portfolio	Internal list that details all the services offered by a service provider, including those in preparation, live and discontinued. Note: For each service, the service portfolio may include information such as its value proposition, target customer base, service description, relevant technical specifications, cost and price, risks to the service provider, service level packages offered, etc.
Service provider	Organization or federation (or part of an organization or federation) that manages and delivers a service or services to customers.
Service request	User request for information, advice, access to a service or a change. Note: Service requests are often handled by the same process and tools as incidents.
Service review	Periodic evaluation of the quality and performance of a service in conjunction with the customer, or under consideration of customer feedback, from which opportunities for improvement are identified, follow-up actions to increase the value of the service are determined.
Service target	Reference/target values for a parameter used to measure the performance of a service, listed in a service level agreement (SLA) related to this service Note: Typical service targets include availability or resolution time for incidents.
Supplier	Organization or party that provides a (supporting) service or service component(s) to the service provider, which the service provider needs to provide services to their customers/users. Note 1: A supplier may be internal or external to the organization of the service provider. Note 2: In a federation, the federation members are regarded as internal suppliers.
Top management	Senior management within an organization who have authority to set policies and exercise overall control of the organization.
Underpinning agreement (UA)	Documented agreement between a service provider and an external supplier that specifies the underpinning service(s) or service component(s) to be provided by the supplier, together with the related service targets. Note 1: A UA can be seen as a service level agreement (SLA) with an external supplier where the service provider is in the customer role. Note 2: A UA may also be referred to as an underpinning contract (UC).
Underpinning contract (UC)	See: Underpinning agreement (UA).
User	Individual that primarily benefits from, and uses, a service.
Value	Benefit to a customer and their users delivered by a service. Note: Value should be considered as a composition of the function (fitness for purpose) and quality (fitness for use, covering sufficient availability/continuity, capacity/performance and information security) connected to a service.

Workaround	Means of circumventing or mitigating the symptoms of a known error that helps to resolve incidents caused by this known error, while the underlying root cause is not permanently eliminated. Note 1: Workarounds are often applied in a situation when the actual root cause of (recurring) incidents cannot be resolved due to lack of resources or ability. Note 2: A workaround may consist of a set of actions to be carried out by either the service provider or the user of the service. Note 3: A workaround is also referred to as a temporary fix or temporary solution.

Appendix D: List of FitSM requirements

FitSM has numbered all requirements. This numbering initially consists of the abbreviation GR or the process abbreviation. This is followed by the numbering of the general requirements or the numbering of the processes. This is in turn followed by numbering within the general requirement or process.

For example, requirement GR 1.2 is the second requirement of the first area in the general requirements. The requirement SLM 2.4 is the fourth requirement in the Service Level Management process, which is the second process in the FitSM sequence.

General requirements
GR 1.1 Top management takes responsibility
GR 1.2 Specify service management policy
GR 1.3 Conduct management reviews
GR 2.1 Document service management system (SMS)
GR 2.2 Create process descriptions
GR 2.3 Document process results
GR 2.4 Control documents
GR 3.1 Identify stakeholder expectations
GR 3.2 Define the scope of the SMS
GR 4.1 Create and maintain service management plan
GR 4.2 Align all plans
GR 5.1 Implement service management plan
GR 5.2 Apply processes in practice
GR 6.1 Measure effectiveness
GR 6.2 Determine SMS maturity level regularly
GR 7.1 Identify and correct target deviations
GR 7.2 Plan and implement improvements

Process requirements

Offer and Agree

CRM 7.1 Identify service customers
CRM 7.2 Establish contact points for customers
CRM 7.3 Establish communication channels for customers
CRM 7.4 Conduct service reviews regularly
CRM 7.5 Handle customer complaints in a uniform manner
CRM 7.6 Manage customer satisfaction
SPM 1.1 Specify and maintain service portfolio
SPM 1.2 Evaluate service proposals
SPM 1.3 Plan design and transition for services
SPM 1.4 Identify organizational support
SLM 2.1 Maintain service catalog
SLM 2.2 Agree and regularly review SLAs
SLM 2.3 Review service performance
SLM 2.4 Agree and regularly review OLAs and UAs
SLM 2.5 Review performance of service components

Plan and Ensure

SUPPM 8.1 Identify internal and external suppliers
SUPPM 8.2 Establish contact points for suppliers
SUPPM 8.3 Establish communication channels with suppliers
SUPPM 8.4 Evaluate suppliers regularly
SACM 4.1 Identify and regularly check availability/continuity requirements
SACM 4.2 Check availability/continuity risks regularly
SACM 4.3 Reduce risks
SACM 4.4 Monitor availability
CAPM 5.1 Identify and regularly review capacity/performance requirements
CAPM 5.2 Identify current capacity and utilization
CAPM 5.3 Plan resources
CAPM 5.4 Monitor and analyze performance

Monitor and Roll-out

RDM 13.1 Define release and deployment strategy
RDM 13.2 Define criteria for including changes in a release
RDM 13.3 Plan acceptance criteria and deployment
RDM 13.4 Create, test and accept releases
RDM 13.5 Plan failure scenario
RDM 13.6: Post Implementation Review
CHM 12.1 Record and classify changes uniformly
CHM 12.2 Define uniform procedure
CHM 12.3 Evaluate changes uniformly
CHM 12.4 Approve changes uniformly

CHM 12.5 Carry out PIR as required and close changes uniformly
CHM 12.6 Maintain schedule of changes
CONFM 11.1 Define configuration items (CIs) and relationships
CONFM 11.2 Define level of detail CI recording
CONFM 11.3 Create and maintain CMDB
CONFM 11.4 Control CIs and monitor changes
CONFM 11.5 Regularly review contents of the CMDB

Eliminate and Prevent
ISRM 9.1 Uniformly record, classify and prioritize incidents/service requests
ISRM 9.2 Resolve/fulfill incidents/service requests according to SLA specifications
ISRM 9.3 Escalate incidents/service requests uniformly
ISRM 9.4 Inform customers and users about progress
ISRM 9.5 Close incidents/service requests uniformly
ISRM 9.6 Identify and handle major incidents consistently
PM 10.1 Identify problems consistently
PM 10.2 Investigate and resolve problems
PM 10.3 Record Known Errors
PM 10.4 Maintain current information on Known Errors

Report and Improve
SRM 3.1 Identify reports
SRM 3.2 Specify reports
SRM 3.3 Create and distribute reports
CSI 14.1 Identify potential for improvement and plan audits
CSI 14.2 Evaluate and implement improvement potentials in a uniform manner
CSI 14.3 Monitor implementation of improvement measures

Protect and Secure
ISM 6.1 Define information security (IS) policies
ISM 6.2 Assess IS risks regularly
ISM 6.3 Implement IS measures
ISM 6.4 Handle IS events/incidents consistently
ISM 6.5 Implement access control in a consistent manner

Index

S

T

U

www.ingramcontent.com/pod-product-compliance
Ingram Content Group UK Ltd.
Pitfield, Milton Keynes, MK11 3LW, UK
UKHW051450290926
15471UKWH00008B/1118